Empowering Your Library

A Guide to Improving Service, Productivity, & Participation

Connie Christopher

AMERICAN LIBRARY ASSOCIATION
Chicago
2003

Composition by the dotted i in Minion and Univers using QuarkXPress 4.1 for the Macintosh

Printed on 50-pound white offset, a pH-neutral stock, and bound in 10-point cover stock by Victor Graphics

The paper used in this publication meets the minimum requirements of American National Standard for Information Sciences—Permanence of Paper for Printed Library Materials, ANSI Z39.48-1992. ⊚

Library of Congress Cataloging-in-Publication Data

Christopher, Connie.
    Empowering your library : a guide to improving service, productivity,
and participation / Connie Christopher.
      p.   cm.
    Includes bibliographical references and index.
    ISBN 0-8389-0858-6
    1. Library personnel management. 2. Employee empowerment. 3. Employee motivation. 4. Library employees—In-service training. 5. Library administration—Employee participation. 6. Communication in library administration. 7. Leadership—Psychological aspects. 8. Management—Psychological aspects. I. Title.
Z682.C55 2003
023—dc21   2003010680

07 06 05 04 03   5 4 3 2 1

Contents

Figures

Acknowledgments

I would like to express thanks to the American Library Association for the opportunity to write about a topic that has held a lifelong fascination for me; my colleagues at Multnomah County Library, who are a constant source of inspiration; Maureen and Kelvin Christopher for all their early lessons in personal empowerment; and O.T. for his support and encouragement in writing this book.

Introduction

WHY EMPOWERMENT AND WHY NOW?

How many times in recent weeks have you read or heard someone say one or more of the following?

> The challenges libraries face increase every day.
>
> We must make choices from an ever-increasing number of priorities.
>
> Technology is speeding things up.
>
> Our customers are expecting more.
>
> The need to learn is ceaseless.
>
> How are we going to replace all the upcoming retirees?
>
> We have to set priorities for spending.
>
> The library business is more complex than ever before.

There is no question that libraries exist in an increasingly competitive world. We are not only competing with other information agencies for customers; we also compete for funding, for staff, and for staff's psychological commitment to the organization's success. All of this is coming at a time when a shortage of librarians is expected in the near future.

We are constantly engaged in the business of improving our services. Libraries today are attempting to *reinvent* themselves to remain viable participants in the information universe. Increasingly, library leaders are looking beyond other libraries for best practices. Library managers talk about improving the overall organization quality and also improved service to customers. At the same time we see the need to be nimble and flexible in adapting to changes dictated by those customers and the external environment.

These requirements translate to increasingly sophisticated and complex staff development needs. Creating an organization where continuous learning and innovation are not only valued but also viewed as essential is critical to the success of your library. We need the hearts as well as the minds of our staff to ensure strong commitment to the long-term viability of our libraries.

At the same time the organization needs are growing, we hear staff talking about the importance of work-life quality for all employees. The significance of work and personal life balance is being discussed openly, particularly by younger librarians. The next generation of library leaders looks to the senior leaders they may someday replace and asks themselves, "Do I want to live like that?"

As the need to focus attention on long-range planning as well as thinking strategically about our mission and our place in the knowledge world grows, we cannot avoid wondering how we will accomplish all of this as the demands for our time, attention, and financial resources continue to increase.

Staff and leadership development will continue to grow in importance, as will learning how to maximize existing staff and other resources. An energized, fully committed workforce is needed to meet the many challenges that libraries face. Empowerment is *not* the management fad of the week but rather a *competitive necessity.* The advantage comes from gaining the ability to fully use the discretionary effort of every employee.

The Case for an Empowered Library

1

The most underutilized resource in many libraries is *staff*. Library employees have a great deal of capacity in their knowledge, experience, and motivation. *Empowerment* is allowing individuals and groups to fully realize their potential. Results include staff gaining new knowledge and skills that produce greater self-reliance. Employees increase confidence in their ability to grow and develop. In doing so they become fully engaged. Staff members feel ownership in the success of the organization. The discretionary effort of the workforce is engaged. Thus the library's resources are fully leveraged. Just as we strive to maximize financial resources, we have the ability to better deploy our library's human resources.

OED Online's definition of *empower* is "(1) to invest legally or formally with power or authority; to authorize, license; (2) to impart or bestow power to an end or for a purpose; to enable, permit; (3) to gain or assume power over."

Empowerment is a relatively simple and often discussed concept. Why is it important in a library setting? Also, if it is an uncomplicated philosophy, why should you devote time to reading about empowerment and planning for developing an empowered staff?

Before we explore empowerment in detail, let's examine the rationale supporting empowering library staff. We read and hear that, although well loved, libraries face threats and major challenges over the coming years. Some argue that the long-term viability of libraries is at stake. This is the library-as-dinosaur scenario.

Regardless of your personal forecast, all agree that significant issues confront information business professionals. Surrounding the urgent need to remain relevant is intense competition for funding, for customers, and for staff. The speed of implementation and the effectiveness of our strategies for maximizing these scarce resources are critical. Greater empowerment of library employees will play an essential role in how your library optimizes formidable challenges resulting from changes in the external world.

COMPETITION FOR FUNDING

The ongoing challenge of library funding is not a new issue. Although it would be pleasant to think of libraries as special places absolved from the conditions in the world around us, libraries must compete for funding with many other worthy entities. Public libraries, though highly regarded in their communities, are often part of government. Thus they share funding with essential services such as police, fire, and health departments. Academic libraries vie for financial resources with other departments within their institution. Resources needed for teacher and administrator salaries, computers, and textbooks affect school library funding.

Other factors affecting library budgets are the status of the economy, the political climate of the country and community, government regulations, and the constituency's perception of the value of library services in relation to other priorities and choices.

To the extent that time and attention are focused on maintaining the library's funding sources, the resource pool available for other work is diminished. Imagine if the library director and three key managers spend one or two days a week for four months fully devoted to work involved in passing a library funding levy or helping shore up a particular funding source. That time is taken away from the basic information delivery business. The time is gone forever. If those library managers are the key players in implementing modifications to the organization's service plan, for example, then core work is not getting done while they are dedicated to funding sources. However, if the library staff is empowered, committed to, and fully engaged in implementing the plan, the temporary siphoning off of the time of four key managers does not slow the library's progress in implementing service initiatives to the extent it otherwise would.

COMPETITION FOR CUSTOMERS

We are no longer sole information providers to our communities. Our patrons have come to rely on search engines like Google and websites such as amazon.com for finding the information previously only available from the library. Online information providers include free-to-consumer, advertiser-paid entities such as askjeeves.com and allexperts.com. Pay-per-search companies—search-on-line.com is an example—charge the consumer for each transaction, with a "next transaction for free if not satisfied" policy.

Libraries compete with these commercial entities and large-scale information providers who market their ability to provide information services to our customers cheaper, faster, and with greater access than we can. Each information access provider, including the library, has a different set of pros and cons related to factors such as cost, ease of access, and service quality for each individual customer. Although libraries will continue to play a role in filling patron needs, alternate information sources will gradually erode the number of customers who depend on the library as a primary information source.

We can expect to lose patrons who can afford home computers, online bookstores, and commercial information services. Library professionals tell you, however, that the library bridges the gap between the information-haves and -have-nots. Although this is true, it is also important to remember that the information-haves, those who are discovering efficient means of meeting their information needs from home, are also taxpayers.

They demand relevance and efficiency from public agencies. How will they feel about their tax dollars supporting libraries, as they themselves use the library less and less?

Excellent customer service pulls all the library's products together and delivers them as a cohesive package (*see* figure 1-1).[1] Items that might be included in a particular customer's service package on a specific day's library visit follow:

Help locating interlibrary loan materials for a genealogy project

Homework help for the fifth-grader

Assistance with government documents for the family business

Story time for the preschool member of the family

Reader's advisory for weekend reading material

The library's reputation is created from opinions resulting from the quality of service customers receive over time, just as your perception of a department store, supermarket, or post office is created over time. Thus the reputation likely evolves from a compilation of a series of transactions or visits. That is, if four of these five transactions are smooth and effortless but the fifth is problematic, it is likely the customer will remember the difficult transaction far longer than he or she will those that were pleasant and without incident. Changes in customer service policies and attitudes at commercial and public agencies over the last two decades have resulted in heightened expectations of all service transactions on the part of library patrons of all ages.

Another critical as well as costly aspect of meeting customer information needs is building, implementing, and maintaining an effective technology plan. Staff time and other resources devoted to equipping library locations with a functional website,

---

FIGURE 1-1 Customer Service Excellence

Excellent service needs to be defined from the customer's perspective. As individuals we understand the importance of providing excellent service to our patrons, but do our actions match our words? Ask yourself these questions to help determine whether your library would thrive in a free market economy.

When was the last time you observed a library patron appear to be in need of assistance while all available employees appear to be engaged in administrative tasks or in conversation with colleagues?

Are your electronic and print resources organized to make them easy to use for customers or to suit staff preferences?

Have you had the experience of observing an excellent customer service practice at a commercial entity and felt a little overwhelmed thinking how long it would take to implement it at your library?

Do our patrons want to know everything about a given topic or just the answer to their questions?

Do we use systems and language the customer can relate to?

Do patrons enjoy navigating our various processes plus physical and personnel peculiarities of each library section?

Do customers see the need to manage these idiosyncrasies as an effective use of their time or a necessary inconvenience?

If customers could accomplish the same end more simply and efficiently from their home offices, would they continue coming to the library?

Do you or people you know use online banking and bill paying and ATM machines? How do these services compare to the convenience of banking hours and services twenty years ago?

Do you remember an earlier era when a department store or supermarket purchase could only be processed in the department from which the product came?

Are there other examples of ways in which commercial or other service entities have adopted new procedures to make their establishments more user-friendly?

Do we take a similar approach to innovation in making it easy for our customers to do business with us?

Or do we think in terms of what is optimal from our perspective?

ample electronic resources, and means for teaching patrons information access continue to grow as the importance of these tools expands.

We have observed significant changes in the expectations of our patrons over the past decade, many driven by technology. What will the next generation of customers expect? In the United States the high school graduating class of 2002 was the first generation never to have touched a typewriter. Their approach to work, learning, and life is different than ours as a result of technology.

For example, usage patterns of students in university libraries differ substantially today from just a few years ago. Unlike students of earlier generations, who may have approached libraries with some apprehension, college students today often approach Internet research enthusiastically. They are able to do a great deal of research without assistance using search engines and hyperlinks. They may or may not be skilled in making qualitative judgments regarding material obtained in their searches. Although the argument made by library professionals regarding the qualitative value librarians might add to this search process is entirely valid, many students or other library users are not aware of either the quality distinctions or of their need for something better. Why would they seek out something they don't know they need?

Thus libraries will continue to formulate and test new strategies of integrating traditional resources with Internet research to support the information needs of this emerging generation of customers. What role will marketing and staff customer service skills play in the work of keeping the library relevant to new generations of patrons? What human and financial resources will be required to meet this challenge?

The increasing use of distance education will require academic libraries to adapt to the distributed environment made possible by new technology. They will also need to improve bibliographic instruction to better meet the needs of users in a customer-friendly manner.

School library media centers will strive to offer a range of programs and services that are competitive with local district and private schools. They must be responsive to changing user information needs and requirements as well as be able to meet students' cultural, social, and behavioral needs.

All librarians need to be capable not only of providing seamless print and electronic reference but also in serving as planner, counselor, manager, teacher, team player, information architect, and collaborator. Librarians who learn skills such as software installation and to perform printer repairs will support their institutions in providing a more comprehensive and competitive customer service package.

As library users are demanding more rapid access to information, the public policy atmosphere becomes increasingly complex. This requires greater individual and organizational competence.[2] Included in such proficiency is the need for more refined analytical, interpersonal, subject, and technical skills in our existing staff. Nimbleness, creativity, and leadership will be required at all levels. It is not only compelling justification for a superb employee development strategy but also for empowerment of all library human resources.

COMPETITION FOR STAFF

Libraries will also be required to compete for personnel. The number of librarian jobs is expected to grow about 5 percent, or 7,000 jobs, between 1998 and 2008. This rate is slower than the average for all occupations. Librarian job openings, however, are predicted at 39,000 for the same period because of retirements and occupation changes.[3] Also significant, the demand growth for qualified and trained information and library personnel from entities other than traditional libraries is increasing fastest. These businesses want workers skilled in managing information, including designing website applications, managing databases, serving as information consultants, and also marketing products to libraries and information agencies.

Average starting salaries for nontraditional librarian careers are significantly higher than those for librarians starting in school, academic, and public libraries, as shown in figure 1-2.

Increasing competition for library school graduates comes at a time when large numbers of traditional librarians and library workers born during the baby boom of the late 1940s through the 1950s will become eligible for retirement. Diverse sources give varying estimates on the number of librarians who will retire in the near future.

To illustrate the impact on libraries created by retiring workers, a 2001 *Los Angeles Times* article stated, "Los Angeles hired 93 entry-level librarians over a recent two year period but lost 92 to retirement and other forms of attrition during the same period. They currently have more than 40 vacancies for rank and file librarians. The situation is similar in Los Angeles County Public Library where 30 of 280 librarian positions are vacant." The same article states:

> City libraries are enjoying a boom, but many veteran staffers are retiring and young ones are lured by the private sector. A decade after Los Angeles slashed spending amid a recession, libraries seem to be back at the top of the city's bestseller list. The pro-

FIGURE 1-2   Librarian Average Starting Salaries

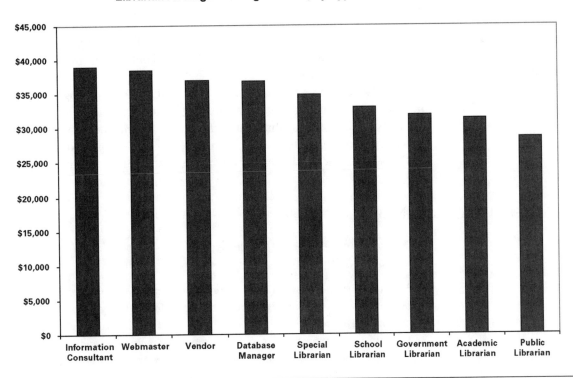

Librarian Average Starting Salaries, by Type of Worker, 1998

Source: "Librarian Employment, by Industry, Projected 2008," *Library Journal* (October 15, 1999): 36–41.

posed budget would boost library spending to a record $68 million to help pay for expanded hours and thousands of new books. The city undertook a major construction program, building five libraries and renovating 30 branches. But beneath the bibliographic boom is a disturbing trend that grates like a stray whisper in a hushed room: Los Angeles is facing a vexing shortage of public librarians. Building more libraries and increasing hours of operation only worsens the crunch.[4]

A few months later, on the opposite side of the country, a *New York Times* story talked about the new, hip librarian image library administrators strive to promote. They are attempting to recruit young people for library school and to fill what may soon be thousands of vacant jobs as older librarians retire and competition for librarians from the private sector intensifies. The article quotes Leigh Estabrook, a professor of the Graduate School of Library and Information Science at the University of Illinois at Urbana-Champaign saying that "about 20 percent of the school's graduates get jobs outside libraries."[5]

The total number of master's degree librarians reported to the National Center for Education Statistics (NCES) in 1990 for academic, public, and school libraries was 97,315 (academic librarians, 26,101 + public, 21,305 + school, 49,909). According to the 1990 census, 197,000 people said they were librarians though only half hold a master's or higher degree, according to Mary Jo Lynch, director of the American Library Association's Office for Research and Statistics. She goes on to discuss possible reasons for differences in reporting for professional versus paraprofessional staff and concludes that because there is no easy way to reconcile the two figures, it is reasonable to use the more conservative number to analyze how many librarians will reach sixty-five in the coming years. Figure 1-3 shows when each of those 87,409 people will reach sixty-five. Figure 1-4 shows the percentage that will turn sixty-five for each five-year period.[6]

Lynch concludes that the shortage reported from coast to coast in 2001 is likely to become more troublesome in the immediate future. Regardless of your definition of *librarian,* the supply-demand forecast indicates a shortage of approximately 25 percent or higher of the current supply of librarians in 2008. The situation will likely be most critical for those school, government, academic, and public libraries in the bottom half of the starting salary scale.

This data also make a compelling argument for maximizing human capacity through empowering existing staff. Library management must allocate time now for the work of developing institutional staff capacity. This includes maximizing existing employee resources as well as recruiting new staff and developing skills necessary to retain the best possible employees, those with and those without library master's degrees.

THE LEADERSHIP CHALLENGE

In the concluding pages of their leadership best-seller, *Primal Leadership,* authors Daniel Goleman, Richard Boyatzis, and Annie McKee tell us:

> Leaders everywhere confront a set of irrevocable imperatives, changing realities driven by profound social, political, economic and technological changes—our world, not to mention the business world, is in the midst of transformational change, calling for new leadership. We face continual increases in computing power, the spread of e-commerce, the rapid diversification of the workforce, the globalization of the economy and the relentless ratcheting upward of the pace—all at an ever accelerating rate of change.[7]

FIGURE 1-3   Number of Librarians Reaching Age 65

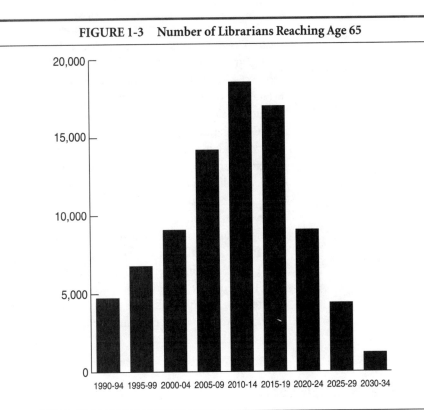

Source: American Libraries (March 2002): 55.

FIGURE 1-4   Librarians Reaching Age 65 (Percentage of 87,409)

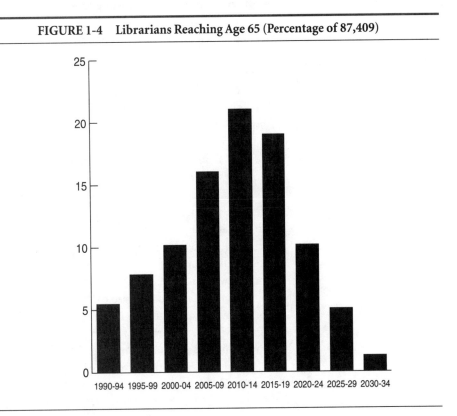

Source: American Libraries (March 2002): 56.

If libraries are to compete successfully, we must transform the way we relate to our customers and the external environment. This dictates effective management of every aspect of the organization in addition to wisely managing financial, physical, and human resources. The process of improvement undergone by libraries in recent years should be a source of pride to all in the profession. We have made significant strides in developing a more efficient or businesslike methodology in our approach to managing libraries.

Consider the work done in areas such as data gathering and statistical techniques, effective resource allocation, strategic planning, decision making, creating sound financial systems, technology planning, intellectual freedom policies, and functional as well as aesthetic building and interior design. These advancements demonstrate library management's vision and ability to effectively embrace change. And yet, how far have these innovations penetrated each of our organizations? Would a more empowered workforce add speed and fresh creativity to the implementation process of each of these initiatives?

In the area of staff development, libraries have begun placing greater emphasis on developing competencies, performance planning and appraisal, teamwork, change management, effective meetings, mentoring, coaching, and succession planning. Would greater ownership of all staff in these processes help us get to implementation more quickly? Would we then be more nimble and responsive to changes in the external environment?

STAFF AS A RESOURCE

Like the building or the collection, staff are also a resource. They are one of the library's most costly resources. According to *Public Library Data Service Statistical Report, 2001,* on average, salaries, excluding benefits, are 52.5 percent of the annual expenditures among all sizes of libraries.[8] The range of salary expense is from 11.7 percent to more than 80 percent. This is the most expensive single category in any library's budget. If fringe benefits were added, the percentage would be significantly higher.

In *The New Planning for Results,* Sandra Nelson says, "It is imperative that staff time and corresponding effort be used as effectively and efficiently as possible. Staff attention should be directed toward activities that are the most important to the library's mission, goals and objectives. However, few library managers really know how much staff time is spent or should be spent on specific activities. Library managers should be aware that allowing staff to underutilize their skills and abilities wastes library resources."[9]

Continually looking for ways to delegate responsibility to staff is a healthy management practice. It fosters entrepreneurial spirit among personnel involved. It frees the manager to move beyond reacting to day-to-day issues and devote attention to intermediate and long-range planning. At the same time, fresh perspective, innovation, and creativity are introduced. The process of delegating makes a major contribution to staff growth and development.[10]

When employees increase ownership in their actions, improved customer service, both internal and external, is the result. If employees feel that they are owners rather than insignificant parts of a larger machine, they can have as much passion for the library's success or failure as the director does.

In summarizing the difference between small business owners and library employees, David Orenstein of Montgomery College in Maryland found, in a series of interviews, that the small business owners described themselves first as business owners, listing their hobbies in third or fourth place. In contrast, the library employees he interviewed identified their hobbies or other interests first when describing themselves. Work was third or fourth in their self-descriptions.[11]

In *Motivating Today's Library Staff*, Dana C. Rooks explains, "While the work itself may be of secondary importance it does not mean that they (staff) cannot be motivated to be committed to the organization and its goals. It is the job of the manager to provide the opportunity for employees to achieve greater satisfaction (in their jobs) rather than seek reward and fulfillment in outside activities." She goes on to suggest that employees be given an opportunity to suggest how job duties can be structured to enhance their fulfillment.[12]

YOU AS A RESOURCE

Personal empowerment or mastery involves creating a strategy for continuous self-improvement and in doing so aligning your skills and value with the library. It includes a personal learning plan allowing you to simultaneously become an indispensable employee and a more fulfilled human being. Part of this self-directed learning may include discovering how to manage transitions effectively, achieve better balance between professional and personal life, and manage projects, in addition to evaluate and manage risks.

Developing personal power is the ability to find your own truth and then create the life you want based on it. It is finding the essence of your self, validating it, and incorporating complete expression of it. David Gershon and Gail Staub list seven sources of personal power: (1) commitment, (2) discipline, (3) support system, (4) inner guidance, (5) lightness, (6) love, and (7) finding your own truth.[13]

Gershon and Staub tell us the majority of our mental programming results from childhood, when we had no filters relative to the helpful as well as unhelpful beliefs we learned from parents, teachers, and other authority figures. As children we uncritically accepted that programming and now, later in life, rarely question it. Most actions today are determined by those core beliefs taken at a young age: (1) attitude toward self-responsibility, (2) self-esteem, (3) trust in the universe, (4) positive attitude, and (5) flowing with change.[14]

The core of personal mastery involves learning to keep simultaneously both a personal vision and a clear picture of current reality. Doing this generates a force within us called "creative tension." Tension by nature seeks resolution. We assimilate the vision consciously and unconsciously. We are not likely to have the ability to command ourselves to snap instantly into this frame of mind. The discipline of personal mastery suggests that we can, as individuals, cultivate a way of thinking that gradually leads us to it. The more we practice this way of thinking, the more we will feel competent and confident.[15]

Personal mastery also teaches us not to shrink back from seeing the world as it is, even if it makes us uncomfortable. Being honest with ourselves and looking closely and clearly at current reality is one of the most difficult tasks of this discipline. As you anticipate the future of libraries and the role you will play in helping shape that world, have you considered personal empowerment in light of your professional and personal goals?

SUMMARY

Major developments in library management over the last ten years include facing the need to be proactive and relevant, now and in the future. We have placed greater emphasis on increasing capacity for meeting constantly evolving customer information needs. We see the necessity of continuous improvement and innovation at all levels of internal and external customer service.

Although a large part of our target audience still sees libraries as repositories of books, we are working hard to embrace and understand technology to help our future customers see us as the information provider of choice. Just as our staff are retiring, so are our patrons. Academic librarian Marianne Afifi maintains, "The users of libraries will determine the future of libraries, just as they have done so over centuries. Children born in 2001 will be elementary school children in 2007 and the college students of 2019. This population will have grown up with the Internet and connectivity. They will demand ubiquitous, personalized and speedy access to information."[16]

She goes on to say that libraries must facilitate the process of information delivery when and where it is needed, whether this is a physical space or using a personal information appliance on an airplane. A large number of people may never even set foot in a library, but at the same time these people may require many of the resources and services made available to them in cyberspace.

The most effective way to maximize existing human resources comes through creating an environment of empowerment. Staff at all levels have ownership in the success of the organization. They are engaged in continuous personal growth, professionally challenged, and committed to excellence. Let's discover more about how that might happen in your organization.

Notes

1. M. Sue Baughman, "Developing a Customer Service Attitude," in *Staff Development: A Practical Guide,* 3d ed. (Chicago: ALA, 2001), 89.

2. Kathryn M. Deiss, "Introduction to Staff Development," in *Staff Development: A Practical Guide,* 3d ed. (Chicago: ALA, 2001), 3.

3. Olivia Crosby, "Librarians: Information Experts in the Information Age," *Occupational Outlook Quarterly* (winter 2000–01): 9–10.

4. Sue Fox, "Shortage of Librarians Stifling Expansion," *Los Angeles Times,* April 30, 2001.

5. John W. Fountain, "Librarians Adjust Image in an Effort to Fill Jobs," *New York Times,* August 23, 2001.

6. Mary Jo Lynch, "Reaching 65: Lots of Librarians Will Be There Soon," *American Libraries* (March 2002): 55–56.

7. Daniel Goleman, Richard Boyatzis, and Annie McKee, *Primal Leadership: Realizing the Power of Emotional Intelligence* (Boston: Harvard Business School Pr., 2002), 246.

8. Public Library Association, *Public Library Data Service Statistical Report, 2001* (Chicago: ALA, 2001), 21–38.

9. Sandra Nelson, *The New Planning for Results: A Streamlined Approach* (Chicago: ALA, 2001), 31.

10. Dana C. Rooks, *Motivating Today's Library Staff: A Management Guide* (Phoenix: Oryx, 1988), 26.

11. David Orenstein, "Being in the Library Business: An Entepreneurship Primer for Library Administrators," *Library Administration & Management* (spring 2002): 83–91.

12. Rooks, *Motivating Today's Library Staff,* 20–24.

13. David Gershon and Gail Staub, *Empowerment: The Art of Creating Your Life As You Want It* (New York: Dell, 1989), 49–65.

14. Ibid.

15. Peter M. Senge, *The Fifth Discipline: The Art and Practice of the Learning Organization* (New York: Doubleday, 1991), 7–8.

16. Marianne Afifi, "Lessons in the Future of Libraries," *Faculty Forum: The Newsletter of the USC Academic Senate, University of Southern California* 2, no. 2 (May 2000–01): 3.

2

Empowerment and the Learning Organization

Empowerment is an often-used buzzword that generates either enthusiasm or disinterest. The meaning may seem ambiguous because the word has been widely used. The idea of empowerment in organizations is an alternative to negative politics, manipulation, bureaucracy, and patriarchal belief systems about management, according to Peter Block. He tells us:

> Empowerment promises to instill in our institutional life the same values of individual freedom, dignity and self-governance that we embrace as a society. One of the failings of our democracy is that our organizations continue to be managed in an autocratic and top-down way despite our espoused belief in the fundamental value of individuals and their right to create paths of their own choosing. . . . We as managers too often operate on the premise that the way to value employees is to take care of them, as a parent would a child. . . . If employees believe they will be taken care of, their sense of personal responsibility and their drive to treat the organization as their own are diminished.[1]

Empowerment gives people greater control over their destiny. When people have authority, resources, information, and accountability, they feel responsible and act responsibly.[2]

How then do you transform your organization into an empowered library? Although we can learn from others, at some point the need to know everything becomes an excuse for not acting. The core of empowerment theory is that the answer lies within ourselves. We need to be experimenters, not researchers.[3]

Thus there is no special or unique formula for implementing personal empowerment. With groups or organizations, however, it involves working with colleagues to develop a shared vision of your ideal empowered library, articulating a formal or informal plan, and building a commitment to make it happen. Meanwhile, cultural conditions such as trust, excellent communication, and clear expectations create a favorable climate for empowerment.

We all have the capacity to experiment and learn. However, our existing organization structures may not be conducive to the sort of reflection and resulting action needed to transform a traditional culture to an empowered one.[4] How might we establish an organization culture and structure that will allow us to create an empowered library?

A climate of continuous learning nurtures these conditions. This is sometimes dubbed the learning organization or, very simply expressed, enlightened trial and error. The essence of the concept is that blaming destroys innovation. An environment of criticism or reproach is not conducive to continuous learning or to empowering employees.

A group of people who collectively enhance their capability for producing the outcome they desire may be called a *learning organization.* Thus careful examination of the literature on learning organizations will be beneficial in creating your plan for an empowered library. More broadly, a learning organization is a group who continuously enhance their ability to create what they want to create. They place priority on noticing, adapting, and learning from change. Rationale for the learning organization states that in a time of rapid change, only those who are adaptable, flexible, and innovative will thrive. To transform itself into a learning organization, a library needs to discover how to tap employees' capacity and commitment to continuous learning.

The ability to learn or to view life and work as learning curriculum enables the individual to learn from most everything in life. As a result, the learner continues to expand his or her capacity for living and for working. Libraries can establish structure and processes that cultivate continuous learning. For example, managers can support a climate where feedback is continuously exchanged between all levels of staff. Employees have a clear, shared vision of the library's goals and values. Staff are able to reflect on and articulate what they are doing and why.

Employees in a critical or blaming environment, conversely, are reluctant to innovate or experiment for fear of making mistakes that result in added criticism or blame. Learning and personal growth are unimpeded in a climate where blame and criticism are the exception rather than the norm.

It is tempting to think staff need someone to point out shortcomings and errors. Most people want to perform well on the job. Staff stand to profit more if the supervisor's time is spent facilitating and supporting their professional growth rather than in finding fault. Most all-substandard performance is not caused by lack of awareness of faults and mistakes but rather by lack of training and such sound management practices as performance feedback and evaluations.

Thus critical, faultfinding behavior is a powerful demotivator. It is also an ineffective use of precious time. Instead, employees at all levels need compassion and support in understanding priorities and expectations as well as in gaining new knowledge and skills to perform effectively.

The learning organization could be viewed as an evolution of participatory management from the 1970s and other business innovations. It is not characterized by type of structure. Teams (*see* chapter 7) often play a major role. The main focus of the learning organization is closely aligning the individual and the organization in such a way that organizational effectiveness needs and individual job satisfaction needs are met at the same time. The emphasis is on developing the ability for both the individual and the organization to adapt and evolve to changes in the external environment.

Leadership scholar Warren Bennis observes:

The higher the stakes, the more opportunities there are for learning—and, of course, the more opportunities there are for failures and mistakes. But as we have seen, failures and mistakes are major sources of vital experience. As virtually every leader I talked with (in writing this book) said there can be no growth without risks and no progress without mistakes. Indeed, if you don't make mistakes, you aren't trying hard enough. But as mistakes are necessary so is a healthy organizational attitude toward them. First, risk taking must be encouraged. Second, mistakes must be seen as an integral part of the process, so that they are regarded as normal, not abnormal. Third, corrective action rather than censure must follow.[5]

The need to control and closely manage the work of staff is replaced by a desire for continuous learning by all employees in the organization. It benefits the entire organization. Learning ranges from job-specific expertise, to the external environment, to the organization itself and its processes. Work is organized so that what can be viewed as contradictory conditions of organizational effectiveness and individual job satisfaction are integrated and both sets of needs concurrently met.

Peter M. Senge's book *The Fifth Discipline* familiarized the world with the concept of the learning organization. The book was identified by *Harvard Business Review* as one of the seminal management books of the last seventy-five years. In it Senge calls the five characteristics of the learning organization "disciplines" because simultaneous pursuit of these powerful concepts is difficult. (*See* figure 2-1.) They require deliberate focus and effort.[6]

The application of the five disciplines results in an empowered organization. It is an organization with greater capacity for pursuing its mission and for adapting to change in the internal and external environment. Members are better able to achieve their potential, a higher level of motivation, and greater professional as well as personal satisfaction.

Continuous learning is not merely keeping busy or attending one course after another. Nor is it about gathering more and more information or doing the same thing over and over, expecting a different result each time.

Libraries can establish structures and processes that cultivate continuous learning. For example, management can support a climate where feedback is continuously exchanged: peer to peer, manager to employee, and employee to manager. Employees are

---

FIGURE 2-1   Characteristics of the Learning Organization

1. *Systems thinking* involves viewing the individual's role as part of a work team. The team is part of the organization. The organization is part of the larger environment. Systems thinking also involves awareness of the interdependency of people, teams, and the organization.

2. *Personal mastery* means that an individual's personal and professional development are viewed as critical to the organization's success. This learning is more than products or services of the organization. It includes interpersonal competence, personal awareness, emotional maturity, and the ethical and moral dimensions of the organization's work.

3. *Mental models* are based on long-standing assumptions and generalizations about how groups operate. These models may be limiting or dysfunctional. They can prevent the individual or organization from learning and growing. In the learning organization mental models are openly shared, challenged, scrutinized, and revised as needed.

4. *Shared vision* emerges from partial visions of individuals and teams. Organization goals, values, and missions are widely shared and owned by all members. This vision results in a higher level of commitment than when the vision is imposed from the top.

5. *Team learning* involves a team improving its processes for greater effectiveness. Teams may also be called departments, units, divisions, and committees.

Adapted from *The Fifth Discipline: The Art and Practice of the Learning Organization* by Peter M. Senge (New York: Doubleday, 1991), 6–10.

encouraged to have a personal vision, and all staff have a clear, shared vision of the organization's goals and values. Employees are involved in learning activities where they can reflect about what they are doing and why.

Richard Boyatzis developed a model of self-directed learning over three decades of work as academic researcher and consultant to organizations. His theory includes five discoveries, each involving a discontinuity. As with personal mastery or continuous learning, sources of information used for identifying the ideal self, real self, and learning agenda (discoveries 1 to 3) are gathered from personal and professional experience, including reflection and feedback. Discovery 4 involves experimenting with new behavior, thought, and feelings, and discovery 5 requires developing trusting relationships that help, support, and encourage each step in the process.[7] (*See* figure 2-2.)

Each discovery requires different amounts of time and effort. Also, the process is not necessarily orderly. Over time, practicing these new habits incorporates them in our new real selves. With changes in the self come changes in aspirations and dreams. Thus the cycle of continuous learning and adaptation results in professional and personal growth.

For library staff continuous learning is critical to renewing the expertise and skills needed to teach and assist customers in the information age. The revolution in information technology demands changes not only in what we learn but also how we learn. We can support our library's long-term viability by reflecting on how we might take a more active role in our own and our organization's learning.

In an empowered library all staff are engaged in the perpetual cycle of creative tension and self-directed learning. Individuals and groups have a constantly evolving vision of who they want to be based on feedback from the internal and external envi-

---

FIGURE 2-2   Boyatzis's Theory of Self-Directed Learning

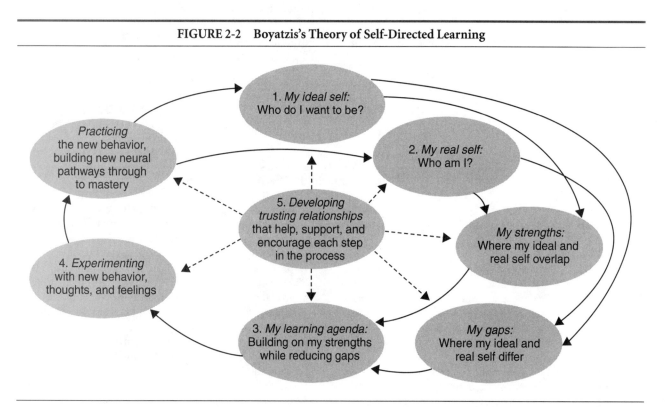

Source: Daniel Goleman, Richard Boyatzis, and Annie McKee, *Primal Leadership: Realizing the Power of Emotional Intelligence* (Boston: Harvard Business School Pr., 2002), 110; and R. E. Boyatzis, "Unleashing the Power of Self-Directed Learning," in R. Sims, ed., *Changing the Way We Manage Change* (New York: Quorum, 2002), 110.

ronment. This cycle of continuous professional growth and development results in greater job satisfaction as well as maximum utilization of library staff. This library is prepared to view the challenges we face as they are, not as we wish they were.

SUMMARY

Although the word itself may be overused and not well understood, *empowerment* offers individuals in organizations many of the values our society cherishes, including freedom, dignity, and self-governance. Rather than treating employees as a parent would a child, organizations need to give employees authority, resources, information, and accountability so they will feel responsible and act responsibly as owners of the organization.

There is no formula for interjecting the experimenting and learning needed to create empowerment in your library or your own life. Continuous learning, however, nurtures these conditions, and thus a study of the characteristics of the learning organization will guide those anxious to create an empowered library.

Senge's *The Fifth Discipline* introduced the world to the concept of the learning organization. He urged organizations to determine how they can encourage employee learning at all levels to re-create themselves and the organization (*see* figure 2-3). Staff in an empowered library are involved in a continuous cycle of creative tension and self-directed learning resulting in continuous renewal and maximum utilization of human resources.[8]

Notes

1. Peter Block, *The Empowered Manager: Positive Political Skills at Work* (San Francisco: Jossey-Bass, 1991/1987), xiii–xiv.

2. Kimball Fisher, *Leading Self-Directed Work Teams: A Guide to Developing New Team Leadership Skills* (New York: McGraw-Hill, 2000), 15–16.

3. Block, *The Empowered Manager*, xvi.

4. Ibid., 20–25.

5. Warren Bennis, *On Becoming a Leader* (New York: Addison-Wesley, 1989), 185.

6. Peter M. Senge, *The Fifth Discipline: The Art and Practice of the Learning Organization* (New York: Doubleday, 1991), 10–11.

7. Daniel Goleman, Richard Boyatzis, and Annie McKee, *Primal Leadership: Realizing the Power of Emotional Intelligence* (Boston: Harvard Business School Pr., 2002), 109–12.

8. Senge, *The Fifth Discipline*, 14.

FIGURE 2-3   Checklist: Is Your Library a Learning Organization?

Think about the following statements in relation to your library. This will be helpful for groups and individuals contemplating staff learning and developmental needs.

___ Most individuals in the organization are growing and stretching their capacity to create.

___ People feel their work matters—both to themselves and to patrons and the community.

___ This organization values the work of a team or group above that of an individual.

___ Most everyone on staff believes the whole of the organization is more important than the parts or different work units.

___ We are encouraged to think and act with a comprehensive, systems approach.

___ Our culture respects and supports an environment of learning.

___ We are encouraged to take ownership of our own learning and development.

___ We are encouraged to learn how to learn.

___ Our environment is rich in constructive personal feedback.

___ The responsibility of senior leaders in this organization is to manage the process whereby new emerging visions become shared visions.

___ Our senior library leaders support the vision of a learning organization.

___ We strive for an empowered workforce, able to learn and perform.

___ Employees are invited to learn what is going on at every level of the organization so they can understand how their actions influence others.

___ Managers take on roles of coaching, mentoring, and facilitating learning.

___ We support just-in-time learning and coaching.

___ We take time to reflect on what we have done and how we can improve.

___ Individuals and teams use action learning. That is, we learn from careful reflection on problem situations and apply new knowledge to future actions.

___ Staff are encouraged to learn about other staff responsibilities, reporting relationships, and work assignments.

___ Employees know what their colleagues are working on.

___ Staff are encouraged to consider their personal assumptions and biases.

___ We feel free to inquire about each others' assumptions and biases as there are few, if any, sacred cows and "undiscussable" subjects in this organization.

___ People treat each other as colleagues. There is mutual respect and trust in the way we talk to each other, and work together, no matter what our positions are.

___ Staff feel free to experiment, take risks, and openly assess the results. No one is blamed for making a mistake.

___ We learn from our failures as well as our successes.

___ Authority in this library is decentralized and delegated.

___ Senior management backs staff decisions.

___ Staff backs senior management decisions.

___ All levels of staff avoid distorting information and blocking communication channels.

___ Staff use active listening.

___ Learning opportunities are incorporated into operations and programs.

___ Learning and communication are effective across levels of our organization.

___ We share information with our patrons and gather feedback and ideas on how we might improve our services.

___ We devote adequate time to planning and learning.

___ We participate in joint learning events with suppliers, community groups, and professional and academic associations.

___ Staff monitor trends outside our library by examining best practices, attending conferences, and keeping up with professional journals and research.

___ We continue to develop new strategies and mechanisms for sharing learning throughout our library.

___ Efficient computer-based information systems support our organizational learning.

___ Staff have ready access to print and electronic information.

___ We document what we are doing so others can take over as necessary.

___ One of the ways we apply what we have learned is through cross-training.

___ No one person is indispensable.

___ We have interdepartmental projects that are just as important as departmental work.

___ Authority at our library is shared.

___ Work groups self-monitor their progress, not senior management.

___ We are in tune with our patrons and customers and provide exactly what they want.

___ Most staff trust each other.

___ We try to learn from our mistakes rather than place blame.

___ Most staff members are self-starters and self-motivated.

___ We understand each other's strengths and how to use them for the good of the organization.

What about Motivation?

3

Employees were seen as a mere input in the production of goods and services prior to 1930. Evidence that attitudes play a greater role than money in employee motivation emerged at that time. The human relations approach to management followed. This management philosophy suggests that the needs and motivation of employees are the primary focus of managers.

All employees have a desire not only to take pride in their work but also to learn, experiment, and improve. Managers and supervisors cannot motivate employees, but they can give up control and dominance. They can also develop conditions that boost self-motivation. Pushing governance down to lower levels in the organization fosters intrinsic motivation and empowerment. The result will be an increase in the sense of responsibility and ownership at all levels in the organization.

Libraries need motivated employees for survival. Do you know what motivates employees at your library? To be effective, managers need to understand what motivates staff in their work environment. Creating conditions that cultivate intrinsic motivation in employees is one of the most complicated roles of a manager because conditions that motivate specific individuals evolve over time. For example, as income increases, money generally becomes less of a motivator. Frequently, as employees get older, interesting work becomes a more important motivator. Adding to this complexity, all members of a given work group will likely have different motivation needs at a particular time.

Facilitating the unleashing of intrinsic motivation plays an important role in empowering library staff. Positive employee motivation results in staff retention, productivity, creativity, and commitment to the organization. Motivated employees assume ownership for their actions and provide enhanced internal and external customer service. If employees feel that they are owners rather than an insignificant part of a large organization, they can have as much commitment to the library's success as the director does.

MASLOW APPLIED

Abraham Maslow's motivation theory, developed in the 1950s at Brandeis University, integrates the work of Freud, Jung, Fromm, and others. Maslow believed that self-motivation is the key to fulfilling basic human needs and that individuals strive to achieve sets of needs. If the physiological needs are reasonably well fulfilled, a second set of needs emerges. The safety needs include security, stability, dependency, protection, structure, order, rules, limits, and freedom from fear, anxiety, and chaos. Satisfaction of these needs eliminates anxieties by ensuring a safe working environment and a reasonably predictable future.

In Maslow's "Hierarchy of Needs," each level of satisfaction is not sought until the previous level has been partially gratified. Once a need level has been satisfied, it is no longer a motivating influence. Based on Maslow's theory, if managers want staff to produce optimal results, they can work to understand employee needs and create conditions conducive to meeting them. (*See* figure 3-1.)

In *Motivating Today's Library Staff,* Dana C. Rooks points out that threats by management to lower-level physical and security needs of staff are often perceived as empty and only serve to alienate employees. They may push staff into proving management wrong. The majority of library employees achieve satisfaction of the first two levels of need within the hierarchy. As underpaid as some claim to be, the salary is sufficient to cover the basics of food, clothing, and shelter. Libraries generally provide a high level of job security and are not influenced by minor economic changes or earnings cycles as corporations are. Employee benefits add to the job's fulfillment of security needs. Rooks asserts the key to motivating library staff is to focus on higher-level needs.[1]

FIGURE 3-1   Maslow's Hierarchy of Needs

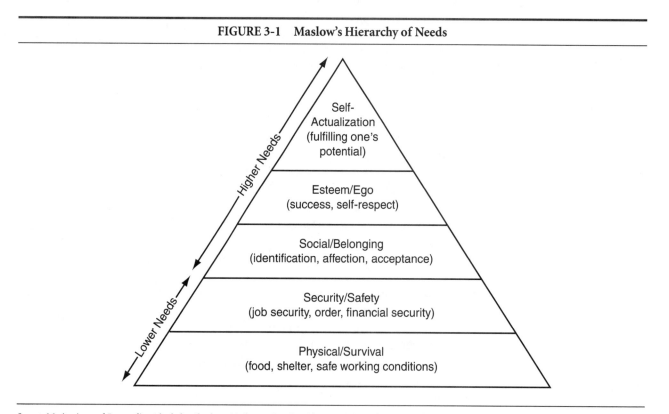

Source: Motivation and Personality, 3d ed., by Abraham Maslow. © Reprinted by permission of Pearson Education, Inc., Upper Saddle River, N.J.

Included in Maslow's third level are social needs including acceptance, camaraderie, and the feeling of belonging. Employees at all levels in the library play an important role in creating and maintaining a welcoming, accepting, emotionally healthy environment for all. This makes a compelling case for managers and supervisors serving as positive role models and also carefully monitoring the way new employees, on-call staff, and volunteers are made to feel welcome. Social needs as well as those in the next levels, "Esteem/Ego" and "Self-Actualization," are enhanced in a learning organization where employees actively seek personal and professional feedback as a means of achieving life and work goals.

Esteem includes the individual's need for self-respect and the respect of others. Fulfillment of the esteem need level results in an individual's sense of self-confidence and personal power. A staff member with healthy self-esteem feels useful and vital to the success of the library. Managers observe conditions that make employees feel confident, useful, and necessary every day. They can then re-create those conditions in a variety of settings to positively influence individual and group motivation. In addition to carefully studying what motivates specific employees, managers may also gather information about rewards and recognition that are meaningful to various staff members.

As an example, one urban public library surveyed staff and found that 90 percent of its employees prefer a simple thank-you for recognition. Forty percent also consider a special reward meaningful. This was followed by 26 percent who considered an award or certificate significant recognition, and only 15 percent who favored special events or ceremonies worthwhile acknowledgment. Clearly, the type of recognition preferred by staff is unique to every organization. Managers benefit from understanding the types of acknowledgment employees in their work groups prefer, particularly because the recognition may not be readily apparent if it varies significantly from the sort of recognition the manager prefers.

Hence the goal of motivation is to create an environment that enables employees to strive for higher-level needs. Although esteem and self-actualization are not the most compelling needs in Maslow's hierarchy, they produce the greatest benefit for the organization and also the individual. These are the needs most often unfulfilled in work and in life. To maximize human resources and empower library staff, managers and supervisors can recognize and cultivate conditions that allow staff to meet their needs and simultaneously enhance the value of the library.

McGREGOR APPLIED

Douglas McGregor, a pioneer in the industrial relations field and a longtime professor at MIT's Sloan School, originated one of the most well known innovations in organization development, known as *Theory X* and *Theory Y*. According to him, effective managers have an optimistic view of human nature, which he called Theory Y.

Theory Y managers believe that motivation comes from within and that people are fundamentally hardworking and responsible and need only be supported and encouraged. Ineffective managers, by contrast, assume people are lazy, resistant to change, and unreliable. Thus they add all kinds of control systems, the paraphernalia of bureaucracy that McGregor called Theory X.

McGregor believed employees are capable and have a desire for professional growth. He said individuals seek control of their own development and want to contribute to the organization's mission. Employees seek rewards and recognition for their accomplishments. Thus McGregor felt the responsibility of management is to create an atmosphere where people can find fulfillment and satisfy their higher-level needs for esteem, recognition, and achievement.[2]

Theory Y emphasizes the importance of self-direction and shares common themes with Richard Boyatzis's cycle of continuous learning and adaptation called "Boyatzis's Theory of Self-Directed Learning," illustrated in chapter 2, figure 2-2. Peter M. Senge's learning organization also focuses on integration of personal and professional development, that is, creating an environment where employees achieve their own goals by directing effort toward success of the organization (*see* chapter 2). The ideas of integration and self-direction inherent in Theory Y, like Maslow's hierarchy, suggest the library will be more successful in achieving its mission if it adjusts and adapts to the needs and goals of its members rather than expecting the opposite.

When McGregor published his classic book, *The Human Side of Enterprise*, in 1960, he told skeptics rather than coming from an ivory tower, his theory was the result of observing and documenting human behavior. Now it is considered fundamental research in the organizational development field. It is also the way knowledge is gained in a learning organization: action learning, learning from experience, learning by doing.

HERZBERG APPLIED

Frederick Herzberg is considered the father of job enrichment and a pioneer in motivation theory. In the late 1950s, he surveyed more than two hundred engineers and accountants. He asked them to think of a work-related incident that made them feel very negative or very good about what happened and then to tell him why it made them feel negative or good. He discovered a commonality of five negative factors and five positive factors, which he called dissatisfiers and satisfiers. The dissatisfiers were

1. policy and administration,
2. supervision,
3. relationship with supervisor,
4. work conditions, and
5. salary.

Herzberg's satisfiers were

1. achievement,
2. recognition,
3. the work itself,
4. responsibility, and
5. advancement.

Despite differences in methodology, there is an interesting relationship between Maslow's lower and higher needs and Herzberg's negative dissatisfiers and positive satisfiers. Achievement and recognition were listed most frequently as motivators, but the respondents reported that the other three factors were longer lasting in their effect. The employee's manager or supervisor has a great deal of impact on the positive motivational factors identified by Herzberg.

In libraries the supervisor generally determines how much responsibility is given to individual staff members and to teams. Management staff have significant impact over conditions that affect the employee's intrinsic motivation as they generally control

work distribution and delegation,

freedom and autonomy,

work challenge and variety,

development and training, and

advancement opportunities.

Creating an atmosphere that enhances motivation is a complex process. Library managers who learn to understand the needs of their staff as well as factors that influence employees' work attitudes and behavior will help facilitate staff motivation. One method of increasing the likelihood of success is to talk with and involve staff in determining criteria for stimulating intrinsic motivation.

LIBRARIES' RECRUITING ADVANTAGE

Library staff generally have a high level of job satisfaction and motivation resulting from the work itself. Both internal and external values impact motivation differences among library staff. Examples include attitudes about entitlement, employer loyalty, importance of life outside the library, family, hobbies and avocations, and the role of satisfying work.[3]

When jobs are relatively easy to obtain, competition among public- and private-sector employers for employees is intense. Given libraries' difficulty in competing for staff based solely on salary, it is important that library recruiters understand their competitive advantage in being able to offer satisfying and meaningful work. If the library is also able to demonstrate its commitment to staff professional development, this will also serve as an added bonus. All of these features can be accentuated in the recruiting process. It is a significant advantage in attracting, retaining, and developing talented staff.

A major overhaul of staff salary scales would be necessary for libraries to compete with businesses for employees. Thus understanding what employees value in their work and accommodating individual differences in motivation and fulfilling work are vital to developing and sustaining a competitive hiring and retention advantage. The key to attracting employees to libraries is to understand their needs and what motivates them.

Libraries can also design work that is based on meeting employee needs and at the same time fulfilling the library's mission. Particularly when the economy is strong and unemployment is low, employees in all job classifications have more employer options. In this environment they may be more interested in employment that fulfills such needs as self-esteem and self-actualization.

This results in a unique opportunity for libraries to market career opportunities that appeal to higher-level needs. If a prospective employee believes job content is more meaningful than salary, and either of several job opportunities at different organizations will meet their lower-level needs, despite some salary variation, the candidate looking for job content is likely to choose the library job.

Managerial competencies should include understanding how to accommodate integration of changing staff work-life values with changing needs of the organization.

Today's new hires are often quite different from their senior colleagues in attitudes, beliefs, and values. They come to the library with more education, there are more two-income families, and the relationship between work and personal life is viewed differently.

Some managers may feel employees with broad interests and goals, personal and professional, may not be capable of devoting adequate attention to library goals. This assumption warrants examination. *Quantity* of work can be confused with *quality* of work. Many employees no longer live their lives for their employer. They do not feel a strong sense of obligation and do not accept organizational goals without question. They expect evidence of value for their commitment to the organization and its mission.

Though their work may be of equal importance to their lives, as a whole, this does not translate to an either-or proposition for the library. Employees can be highly motivated as well as committed to contributing quality work. In this setting the manager understands the employees and creates opportunities for them to achieve satisfaction in their library work that parallels that gained in outside activities. The primary focus of the learning organization is closely aligning the individual and organization in such a way that the organization's effectiveness needs and individual job satisfaction needs are met at the same time.

Library managers must consider all the resources available to them for attracting, retaining, and developing high-quality human resources. Employees who view their jobs as fulfilling are also more likely to be committed to the quality of what they produce. Strategies for adding value to a job include

work that also helps achieve personal goals;

support for intrinsic rewards, such as accomplishment or self-worth;

accomplishments reinforced through recognition or other meaningful criteria; and

special projects that bring new skills and expertise in a special interest area.

According to J. Richard Hackman, professor of social and organizational psychology at Harvard University, three psychological states that elicit internal work motivation are (1) meaningful task, (2) full responsibility for the work, and (3) knowledge of the results that is immediate and accurate (*see* figure 3-2).[4]

Understanding effective methods of motivation can also prove extremely beneficial in helping to resolve staff interpersonal problems. The initial step is to analyze the problem. If motivation or morale is the issue, motivation theory may be useful (*see* figure 3-3).

FIGURE 3-2   Job Characteristics That Foster Internal Work Motivation

Task Characteristics		Psychological States		Outcome
Skill variety Task identity Task significance	⇨	Experienced meaningfulness	⇨	
Autonomy	⇨	Experienced responsibility	⇨	Internal work motivation
Feedback from the work itself	⇨	Knowledge of results	⇨	

Source: Work Redesign by J. Richard Hackman and Greg R. Oldham. © Reprinted by permission of Pearson Education, Inc., Upper Saddle River, N.J.

FIGURE 3-3   Applying Motivation Theory to Staff Interpersonal Issues

Ask yourself the following questions to better understand and manage motivation in your work group.

Can work be restructured to produce greater recognition or esteem?

Will organizing staff in smaller work groups increase cohesiveness and decrease the sense of isolation?

Can initiative be encouraged rather than stifled?

Performance versus "presenteeism"—do long hours necessarily equal quality work?

Will delegating help staff prove competency and unique talents in addition to improving morale?

Is this the right job for the right person?

Are employees trusted to make their own decisions and their own mistakes?

Is excessive competition among staff destroying morale?

Are library employees informed of new developments and how their work is affected?

SUMMARY

Motivation is critical for empowered library staff. Managers need to understand how to create an atmosphere conducive to employee motivation. The benefits of motivation are staff retention, productivity, creativity, and commitment. Staff who feel like owners of the library have a great deal of commitment to the organization's success.

Motivation is not clearly understood. Often, conditions conducive to enhancing staff motivation are poorly managed. Effective managers understand how to create conditions that enhance employees' intrinsic motivation and thus their ability. They can choose to yield power with the intent of creating a stronger organization with leadership valued at every level.

Employee development is both rewarding and at times frustrating. An adage of motivational theory says a manager cannot motivate another person without the cooperation and participation of that individual. Motivation is an internal, self-directed drive. Or, to paraphrase an old saying, "You can lead a horse to water, but he won't drink unless he is thirsty." However, this doesn't mean you can't add a little extra salt to his food.

Developing a motivated, empowered organization could be likened to developing effective purchasing expertise. This expertise is defined as learning to obtain excellent value when acquiring supplies, materials, and equipment. In the case of personnel, it is fully utilizing the value of the library's payroll expense. Libraries leverage existing resources in investing time to cultivate an empowered, motivated staff. The payoff is both immediate and lasting. The result is similar to building a financial endowment. Motivated staff build great library legacies. Consequently, the front-end effort not only fully utilizes today's resources but also builds organizational capacity well beyond the work life of the individuals involved.

Notes

1. Dana C. Rooks, *Motivating Today's Library Staff: A Management Guide* (Phoenix: Oryx, 1988), 6.

2. Douglas McGregor, *The Human Side of Enterprise* (New York: McGraw-Hill, 1960), 47–48.

3. Rooks, *Motivating Today's Library Staff,* 20–26.

4. J. Richard Hackman, *Leading Teams: Setting the Stage for Great Performances* (Boston: Harvard Business School Pr., 2002), 95–96.

4

Excellent Communication

An empowered library requires effective individual and group communication. This includes speaking, writing, and active listening. Although all departments and work groups receive direction from library goals and objectives, communication links the groups and the work of meeting the needs of library stakeholders. Excellent communication is essential for continuous learning.

What is excellent communication? *Communication* is not an easy word to define, nor is it an easy skill to master. Strong organizational communication suggests quality, consistency, and quantity. That is, content should be easy to understand. The message is consistent both for clarity and also to engender trust. A variety of means, the quantity, of communication are used, including formal meetings and presentations, memos, frequently asked questions (FAQs), videos, informal gatherings, e-mail, newsletters, one-on-one or small group meetings, and the library intranet. When the same message comes from many sources, it is more likely to be heard and understood (*see* figure 4-1).

Much of the work of library managers and supervisors involves communication. Included are planning, leading, delegating, organizing, and facilitating. Excellent communication includes taking the time to explain the library vision in clear, understandable language. The importance of "walking the talk" cannot be emphasized enough relative to communication. "Walking the talk" could also be called "leading by example" or the reverse of "do as I say, not as I do." As an example, if a senior manager does not explain performance expectations to his or her direct reports in clear, easily understood terms along with encouraging clarifying questions, will the managers or supervisors who report to this senior manager believe this is an institutional priority in working with the groups they supervise? What is the outcome of an organization-wide lack of understanding of performance expectations? Poor communication demotivates employees, stalls progress, and may result in library employees failing to achieve their goals.

How are specific messages best communicated? Options include phone, e-mail, in person, through a formal presentation, at a meeting, or over lunch. A face-to-face meeting provides an opportunity for immediate feedback. It is the richest medium because

FIGURE 4-1   Analyzing Work Group Communications

When analyzing the skill level of your work group or organizational communication, it may be helpful to ask yourself the following questions. Too many yes answers may mean your work group would benefit from additional training in effective communication skills.

Do bad feelings, organizational problems, destructive conflict, and inefficiency result from the way people communicate with each other?

Do we glorify a Western-style (i.e., outgoing, aggressive, expressive, John Wayne–type) approach? Children often learn confrontational, negative language before they learn to play well with others.

Do we get involved in discussions or arguments oriented more toward winning or being right than solving problems?

Is the so-called personality conflict a convenient phrase that allows everyone to avoid responsibility for negotiating interpersonal problems?

Do we have teams that don't work well because team members lack the necessary communication and consensus-building skills?

Are our meetings ineffective because people don't interact effectively?

Does blaming language elicit defensiveness? Would offering to help be more effective in group problem solving?

---

the recipient hears the message and sees the nonverbal cues that are being communicated. It is also the best medium for delegating, coaching, disciplining, instructing, sharing information, answering questions, and checking progress toward objectives. In addition, face-to-face communication supports developing and maintaining interpersonal rapport.

If a message has a great potential to be misunderstood or is ambiguous, then a face-to-face interaction is preferred. When the message is clear and well defined and all involved have a similar understanding of the background issues, then written communication is appropriate. Unlike the spoken word, e-mail affords additional time to develop thoughts and ideas. It is ideal for rapid exchanges of information in a work group where members know each other well. A single message can be communicated to many people simultaneously. It also works well when employees have different schedules or work in different locations. When used effectively, it is efficient.

Each individual's communication manifests itself in many ways. It is the essence of social interaction. It plays a large role in the impression one makes on others. Communication influences self-esteem, assertiveness, and social adjustment. And most important, it takes lots of practice. Considerations for individuals include the following:

Think simplicity. Unfocused, run-on sentences; acronyms; and buzzwords create confusion. The more often jargon is repeated, the less clear the meaning. Use metaphors, analogies, and examples. Communicate complex ideas simply and effectively.

Look for ways to repeat key messages often. A good place to do this is in meetings and such group communications as e-mails and memos.

Again, remember to "walk the talk." If you do the opposite of what you say, loss of credibility generally results. For example, if you say, "We want to develop a trusting and empowered organization," you need to demonstrate that attitude. Give employees support in implementing their ideas if they are consistent with the library plan. If you say, "We want to improve service to internal and external customers," managers and supervisors need to remember that employees are their internal customers and thus be attentive to staff concerns and respond to requests for information within an acceptable period of time.

Address inconsistencies clearly. If there is a legitimate reason, explain it. If there is not, be prepared to explain that too. If you don't feel library management needs to be accountable, don't be surprised if employees adopt the same attitude.

Listen and be listened to. Communication goes two ways. Explain the vision and ask for feedback to ensure staff grasp the message. Don't forget that people at all levels of the organization have to implement the vision. They need to understand and believe in it before it is real for them.

Listening is an active process rather than simply absorbing what the other person says. It involves asking questions when you don't understand as well as reading both verbal and nonverbal cues (*see* figure 4-2). Listening builds rapport and solidifies working relationships.

Communication is one of the most important aspects of leadership as it influences our ability to inspire others. It affects how we articulate the vision of the library, the work unit, or of a specific project or assignment. Good interaction is not agreement but rather when clarity or common understanding is reached.

Consider the situation where the heads of work groups need to communicate upcoming changes in the library's organizational structure. One manager in this situation might choose to send a memo or e-mail to the group. The other manager decides to get the workers together, explain the changes, and answer as many questions as possible. Which method was the most productive? One argument says the written message was faster and more efficient. It can be referred back to as needed. However, if the work group who received the written message spent a great deal of time talking among themselves and second-guessing, it might be concluded that the personal meeting was the most effective and efficient.

There is no right answer in this situation. The best method depends largely on the interpersonal dynamics and state of the working relationships of the individuals involved. Either way, it is essential that group members feel comfortable asking clarifying questions and for additional information. This two-way communication is the essence of active listening.

To develop the idea of active listening, communication can be analyzed as a two-phase process. In the transmission phase the message is sent. The sender decides what the message will be and how it will be sent. In the feedback phase the receiver responds to the message. This may also include a verification and request for additional information. If the process is not done skillfully, the receiver might feel there is no opportunity for feedback or to ask questions. Not only does this impact the quality of the communication but also it has implications for trust between the parties.

FIGURE 4-2 Four Steps of Active Listening

1. Listen for the story. Get rid of distractions. Look, don't stare, at the other person. Allow him to tell the story his own way. Make it seem the other person is all that matters at the time. Let him finish what he has to say. Listen for unvoiced emotions or what is different.

2. Acknowledge and encourage the other person with your body language, such as a head nod or a slight smile. Stand in her shoes while she is talking. Acknowledge the legitimacy of her reality, not "You shouldn't worry about that." Empathize.

3. Probe for clarification. Ask the person for more detail to help him work through the issue. Ask what else he has considered or how he feels about it. Question assumptions. Summarize well.

4. Respond thoughtfully based on what you heard. Put your own agenda aside. Put yourself in the other person's place.

Perceptions surfacing during communication are inherently subjective. People's personalities, values, attitudes, moods, experience, and knowledge influence perceptions. Thus subjective perception influences how messages are sent, received, and interpreted by people involved in a communication loop.

Effective communication may be hampered by these perception biases. Stereotypes and biases cause people to communicate less effectively with some people or fail to communicate specific information for fear of the reaction. As an example, an employee might not share information about an important piece of customer feedback with a supervisor or colleague for fear of the person's anger—otherwise known as "killing the messenger." If this happens, important information does not get forwarded, and communication channels weaken. Over time, this type of behavior will exacerbate personal as well as work-group dysfunction. Instead, staff should be focusing on actual behaviors, knowledge, skills, and abilities.

Much of the message we communicate comes from nonverbal communication. Facial expressions, body language, and even style of dress influence perception and can be misunderstood. It is helpful to be aware that your expressions or body language may convey a message different from what you intend. For example, if a colleague reads or looks away when talking, this may be interpreted as divided attention. The other person may feel he is not being taken seriously or that his ideas are not important. People who fail to respond to a greeting are often thought of as unfriendly or unapproachable rather than preoccupied or shy. Failure to make eye contact during conversation can be viewed with suspicion or uncertainty. We wonder what the person is hiding. Glaring can be interpreted as anger, fear, or avoidance.

In a group setting many behaviors help facilitate excellent communication. Those include the following:

Asking probing questions

Paraphrasing, bridging, and summarizing

Redirecting questions or comments

Giving positive reinforcement

Engaging less-talkative members

Encouraging divergent views

Shifting perspective

Many excellent resources are available for building knowledge and skills in effective communication. Those range from printed materials to one-on-one support. Many libraries use the services of external consultants, coaches, or internal trainers to build staff communication skills expertise.

SUMMARY

Excellent communication is necessary to foster a learning organization and employee empowerment. All aspects of effective communication—including speaking, listening, and writing—require discipline and ongoing practice. It is important that key messages are repeated often through a variety of means, both written and verbal. It is important also to be aware of the impact of nonverbal communication.

Excellent communication is a multifaceted process that requires both parties to have an opportunity to ask questions and give feedback (*see* figure 4-3). This is essential both for trust and also for continuous learning. Consistency between one's actions and words (i.e., "walking the talk") builds strong communication as well as trust between individuals and groups.

FIGURE 4-3   Checklist: Excellent Communication

___ I practice active listening.

___ Our library shares information by a variety of means.

___ I take the time to explain or seek out additional information to provide clarity if someone doesn't understand me or if I do not understand him or her.

___ I understand the importance of "walking the talk."

___ When I talk with my supervisor, peers, or subordinates, I do not allow unnecessary distractions or interruptions to interfere.

___ I understand that excellent communication between people does not necessarily mean they agree on everything.

___ I work at communicating to be understood.

___ External customers and people I work with think of me as friendly and approachable.

___ My communication with others is generally not confrontational.

___ I don't allow personality conflicts to develop with people I work with.

___ I do not engage in blaming or faultfinding behavior.

___ If I am in a meeting that is not effective, I try to help get it on track.

___ I look for nonverbal cues to better understand another person's message.

___ I am skilled at disagreeing with a colleague without engaging in unproductive conflict.

___ I understand that the world would not be a better place if everyone else were more like me.

5

Creating Shared Vision and Trust

WHAT IS SHARED VISION?

Shared vision could be called shared purpose or organization strategy. It is understood and owned by everyone in the library. Why is shared vision necessary? Most important, it is a powerful motivator. Sharing information and communicating broadly build on excellent communication and nurture a trusting workplace culture.

The next phase of creating the empowered learning organization involves shaping a shared organizational vision. Gaining employees' understanding and support is only part of this process. Staff energy and commitment are needed as well to fully utilize a library's human resources.

With shared vision a team works with confidence in each other's direction and purpose. Staff have an excellent grasp of the challenges faced by their library and libraries in general. Each day all are willing to take steady, tangible steps toward larger goals. Knowledge is widely shared, and problem solving is everyone's work. All staff have ownership in the success of the library just as if it were an employee-owned, for-profit enterprise. Managers can be confident knowing teams will not get frustrated or devote valuable time to work that does not support the library's vision. Shared vision supports accountability and thus the library's full resource utilization.

An authentic shared vision evokes the commitment of staff throughout the organization. The vision is not really shared unless it has staying power and energy that lasts for years. It should move library employees through a continuous cycle of action, learning, and reflection. Peter M. Senge, Art Kleiner, Charlotte Roberts, and others assert, "A vision is only one component of an organization's guiding aspirations. The core of those guiding principles is the sense of shared purpose and destiny, including all of these components:

Vision: an image of our desired future

Values: how we expect to travel to where we want to go

Purpose or mission: what the organization is here to do

Goals: milestones we expect to reach before too long"[1]

HOW TO CREATE SHARED VISION

There are a number of ways to create shared vision, but the strategies need to be developmental. Each stage builds the listening capacity of senior leaders and the leadership competence in the entire group. Figure 5-1 lists the five potential starting points for this process. Every organization is currently predisposed to one of them.[2]

You may want to consider selecting a starting point that best fits the practical realities of your library, and gradually, over time, move away from the authoritarian "telling" model toward the empowered "co-creating." The resulting vision will be widely shared. Staff are more willing to devote time, energy, and commitment to the success of the library if they have personal ownership in the planning process.

As small work groups or teams begin the visioning process, it is helpful to create a forum for individuals to also share their personal visions. This forum brings out various personalities, concerns, and unique qualities of team members. It solidifies teamwork and sets the stage for additional collaboration and group visioning. Through connecting to individuals' personal visions and aspirations, people are able to connect their life work to the project itself, again resulting in increased ownership and empowerment. For example, when individual library staff members fully grasp the vision of the library, they experience a sense of excitement in seeing parts of the work where they will be able to make a contribution while growing personally at the same time.

The work of creating shared vision will flow much more smoothly if a sense of trust exists among staff members. Included is trust between employees and management and between work groups, teams, and departments.

FIGURE 5-1   Creating Shared Vision—Developmental Strategies

Shared vision strategies should be developmental based on the current practices in the library culture. Every stage builds the listening capacity of the top leaders and the leadership competence of the remainder of the organization. Telling is the first, least-complex stage. Once a level is accomplished, leaders can move together to the next stage.

Telling	The library director knows what the vision should be, and the organization needs to follow it.
Selling	The library director knows what the vision should be but needs the organization to buy in before proceeding.
Testing	The library director has an idea about what the vision should be, or several ideas, and wants to know the organization's reactions before proceeding.
Consulting	The library director is putting together a vision and wants creative input from the organization before proceeding.
Co-creating	The library director and staff, through a collaborative process, build a shared vision together.

Adapted from *The Fifth Discipline Fieldbook* by Peter M. Senge, Art Kleiner, Charlotte Roberts, et al. (New York: Doubleday, 1994), 314–26.

Many internal and external resources are available to support the work of your organization in the visioning process. Some groups prefer to use a trained, internal or external, facilitator to move groups along and pay attention to process issues. As preparation, some of the questions you will want to consider are those that help staff think about current reality as well as a vision of the future. Peter Drucker suggests asking yourselves the following five questions:

1. What is our business (mission)?
2. Who is our customer?
3. What does the customer consider value?
4. What have been our results thus far?
5. What is our plan?[3]

From your answers to these questions, pull together a shared vision (*see* figure 5-2). Analyze and discuss questions, pull out common themes, and synthesize elements of the discussion possibly by turning the group's attention to agreeing on simple statements that capture shared vision and purposes. Discuss the question, What is the best way to meet customer needs with the available resources? Develop goals, objectives, and an action plan to meet those customer needs.

FIGURE 5-2   Checklist: Shared Vision

___ I understand the vision of the library as a whole.

___ I have a good understanding of why we allocate resources the way we do.

___ We have a strong understanding of our (internal and external) customer needs.

___ We know how well we are meeting those needs.

___ We have a strong understanding of the challenges (internal and external) faced by our library.

___ We have a good grasp of the reputation of our library in our community.

DEVELOPING TRUST

OED Online's definition of *trust* is "to have faith or confidence; to place reliance; to confide in, to, of, on, upon."

To help create context for considering the issue of organizational trust, think about a person with whom you have a trusting relationship. What are the attributes or unspoken rules of your association? Qualities of trust include the following:

Knowing you can share feelings, emotions, and weaknesses having confidence the other person will respect and not take advantage of you

Being vulnerable while believing the other person will maintain your confidence and continue to treat you in a fair, open, and honest way

Assuming the other person will not intentionally belittle or shame you if you make a mistake or admit you do not know something

Providing caring, concern, and mutual respect to assist each other in growing and maturing independently

Individuals vary greatly in their abilities to build relationships and to trust. Those who find trusting difficult often share common themes from the past:

Having been chronically put down for feelings or beliefs

Low self-esteem or feelings of unworthiness caused by past relationships where one was belittled, ignored, or misunderstood

Having been reared in an emotionally or physically unpredictable or volatile environment often created by another who is more powerful

Unresolved grief caused by loss of a loved one or acrimonious divorce, separation, or end of a relationship

Building trust in an organization is similar to building trust between two people (*see* figure 5-3). It includes being as good as your word, sharing information, and following through on commitments. Trusting behavior uses language that conveys acceptance of individual differences and willingness to negotiate and compromise. If a reward, assignment, special activity, or difficult conversation is promised, follow through. Some people distrust the best excuses. Deal with noncompliant behavior consistently. Get back to people if you find you will not be able to follow through.

Enlist staff in as much decision making as is realistic. Prepare employees in advance for change as much as possible. Surprise can escalate negative actions in those who have difficulty trusting. Library employees value information and knowledge, including understanding context and details related to impending changes. They value the opportunity to ask questions and share input.

If a manager or supervisor thoughtlessly uses intimidating actions or statements as a form of behavior control, staff may respond out of fear. The price of such intimidation is high. It sends a message that using fear as a way of urging those less powerful than you to be submissive is acceptable. Retaliation, overt or covert, is a real possibility when intimidation or fear is used as a motivational tool.

It is important to consider that failure in building trust is rarely a result of poor ethics or bad intentions. Trust is destroyed more often by thoughtless behaviors: not getting back to people, failing to consult key stakeholders, overly focusing on your own obligations, and not being considerate of others. We have demanding and busy personal and professional lives. It is more common to see people acting in trust-diminishing ways largely because of daily job pressure and deadlines rather than a sense of malice.

What can be done in the workplace to build a sense of trust? Positive peer and supervisory role models have a significant impact on others. Do you know library employees who are particularly articulate about hope in the goodness of mankind, self-acceptance, and faith in the fairness of life? Find ways to let those people serve

---

FIGURE 5-3   Building Trust

If you or someone you are mentoring lacks trust in an individual or a specific set of circumstances, what steps might improve the situation? You can start by asking these questions:

Do I lack trust in a person or an institution? Which one? How does the lack of trust play out?

Why do I lack trust? What beliefs are behind the lack of trust?

Does a new behavior trait need to be acquired to develop trust?

What would you and would you not be willing to do to change?

---

as positive examples to staff. Encourage informal conversations about trust. Talk about your own fears and times when you have been successful in letting go of fear. Model risk-taking behavior and self-disclosure of negative scripts. If one person demonstrates these behaviors, others will observe the lack of negative consequences and be more likely to experiment with similar conduct.

Warren Bennis believes that "trust is an underlying issue not only in getting people on your side, but also in having them stay there." He believes leaders have four qualities that generate and sustain trust:

1. *Constancy.* Whatever surprises leaders themselves may face, they don't create any for the group. Leaders are all of a piece; they stay the course.

2. *Congruity.* Leaders "walk their talk." In true leaders, there is no gap between the theories they espouse and the life they practice.

3. *Reliability.* Leaders are there when it counts; they are ready to support their coworkers in the moments that matter.

4. *Integrity.* Leaders honor their commitments and promises.[4]

Organizational trust is created by openness. This includes sharing information broadly and giving all employees a mechanism for input and for asking clarifying questions. Staff need to understand why we do things a certain way and the internal and external challenges the organization and libraries in general face. They need to understand the organization's reality in clear and honest terms. Employees require trustworthy role models in how one learns from mistakes.

In *The Fifth Discipline Fieldbook,* Charlotte Roberts discusses a concept called organization intimacy. It starts with the pledge to get to know colleagues beyond their work roles. Members of an intimate team are open about beliefs, feelings, and aspirations. This intimacy suggests vulnerability and a willingness to pass on honest information. It involves being mentally, emotionally, and socially exposed. In an intimate work group, individuals are not free to sneak things by, to withhold information, to pretend to know something they don't, or to propose and implement self-serving policies that undermine team goals.[5]

The lack of trust prevalent in many organizations is not caused by of lack of intimacy but rather is a symptom of it. Building intimacy requires time and attention in the beginning, but it soon leads to immense time savings. People who understand each other intimately waste less effort. They do not have to engage in second-guessing or guard against the attacks of others. Decision quality increases, resulting from truth telling and commitment to shared purpose.[6]

Employees at every level need honest and regular performance feedback. A trusting work environment rich in formal and informal feedback, at every level, rarely results in staff complacently watching others struggle to complete their work. Instead, experienced members readily support and assist colleagues who are still learning.

Share information and communicate broadly. Withholding information conveys many messages. The most critical is lack of trust. People need information to act responsibly. Regardless of an employee's position at the library, he or she makes hundreds of decisions in the course of a workday. Most of these decisions require an element of judgment. The more information and trust the employee has, the better-quality decision he or she will make. Hundreds or thousands of daily high-quality small decisions based on trust in each other and in the organization result in an empowered workforce, a library fit to triumph over a multitude of internal and external challenges.

SUMMARY

The process of creating a shared vision clarifies the mission of the library. It also builds motivation, commitment, and ownership. Other benefits include aligning and focusing individual and group efforts in addition to helping build enthusiasm. A shared vision guides employees through a continuous cycle of action, feedback, learning, and reflection.

As individuals and groups do the work of creating a shared vision, it is useful to analyze the level of trust in the library (*see* figure 5-4). A sense of trust supports the work of developing a learning organization, and it also is more efficient. People who trust each other waste less time and effort on unproductive behavior.

FIGURE 5-4   Checklist: Organizational Trust

Use the checklist as a guide to whether your organization or work group needs to work on building trust.

___ There is a high level of trust between all employees at our library.

___ We demonstrate trust between management and nonmanagement employees.

___ Following through on commitments is a priority in our organization.

___ Staff at this library are strong role models when it comes to valuing individual differences.

___ We talk openly about fear and the ability to let go of it.

___ We are encouraged to get to know each other as people, beyond our job functions.

___ Formal and informal performance feedback is part of our work life at this library.

___ Noncompliant behavior is dealt with consistently at our library.

___ Staff at our library are encouraged to give input and be a part of decision making.

___ I do not use intimidation to control or motivate others.

___ Sharing information and helping people understand the rationale behind changes is important at our library.

___ I model risk-taking behavior.

___ People I work with think of me as trustworthy.

___ I ask questions or seek additional information when I do not understand a decision or a request.

Notes

1. Peter M. Senge, Art Kleiner, Charlotte Roberts, et al., *The Fifth Discipline Fieldbook: Strategies and Tools for Building a Learning Organization* (New York: Doubleday 1994), 302–3.

2. Ibid., 312–26.

3. Peter F. Drucker, *The Five Most Important Questions You Will Ever Ask about Your Nonprofit Organization: Participant's Workbook* (San Francisco: Jossey-Bass, 1993), 10.

4. Warren Bennis, *On Becoming a Leader* (New York: Addison-Wesley, 1989), 160.

5. Senge et al., *The Fifth Discipline Fieldbook*, 70–72.

6. Ibid., 71.

The Manager's
Role

In an empowered library, employees working in teams carry out significant portions of the work done by managers and supervisors in a traditional hierarchical organization. Examples include developing policies, overseeing projects, creating new programs, and long-range planning. The shift in the manager's role from one of command and control to that of facilitator and resource provider is smoother and less threatening if managers clearly grasp and support empowerment and how the benefits of fully utilizing human resources apply to the library's long-term viability.

It is also helpful for employees to understand that empowering staff is not intended to result in job loss but rather in the ability to leverage existing library staff. A starting point in minimizing resistance might be an overview of empowerment rationale in addition to guiding individuals in creating a personal vision of specific new roles and responsibilities. Once all employees grasp the concept that there is more than enough work for all, that the emphasis is merely shifting to maximizing resources, they are likely to be more open to the idea of becoming engaged in the process.

All staff should be involved in some aspect of planning. Thus can they view their expanded role as it benefits the library's long-term survival and its mission as well as their own personal and professional development. Additional compelling personal benefits for staff engaged in the empowerment process include their own long-term job security and general employability. That is, their participation will result in new attitudes and skills that will make them more professionally versatile, both within the library and in the external job market.

In *The New Planning for Results,* Sandra Nelson encourages managers to think differently about who does what in the library:

> The general rule is to assign work to the lowest staff classification capable of doing the work. Not only does this practice benefit the library but it also usually makes the work more interesting and challenging for staff. Although such assignments might be difficult in libraries subject to collective bargaining agreements and in systems that favor tight job descriptions, changes can be made with patience and persistence, especially if staff want opportunities to learn new skills and to have their jobs enriched.[1]

To restate her point, changes will be easier if staff want those opportunities. Managers play a major role in helping staff see the personal and professional benefits of empowerment.

COORDINATING AND FACILITATING

The manager's job is not to manage the work of teams but rather to get the team established and facilitate minor adjustments as the project progresses. Leaders cannot make a team perform well. They can assist in creating and supporting conditions that make the team's success likely. Though initially this approach can be more challenging than managing the team, the end result is often a higher-quality product, morale is better, and team members have learned to better manage their own work. Team processes will be covered in chapter 7.

Empowerment is an evolutionary process. The manager needs to be an astute observer of staff's individual and group progress in the empowerment process. The manager or supervisor must be willing to gradually give up control of portions of the work as employees are ready to assume greater responsibility.

It may be helpful to remember that staff will likely be ready to take on new roles and responsibilities before the manager perceives they are. Initially, giving up control may be difficult for the manager, so being aware that this may happen will smooth the process. Yielding control should not be confused with abdication of responsibility. The manager is present and plays a coaching, rather than a directing, role.

The manager assumes a primary role in determining the scope of the work to be done. However, providing too much direction on *how* the work is done can be a powerful demotivator. If *how* rather than *what* becomes an issue between managers and teams, it may help the manager to reflect on both the role of his or her own ego and the degree of perfection needed for this particular work. There are times when letting go of the details and trusting staff to find their way, though somewhat different from our way, may require faith and patience.

This does not mean the work will be inferior but merely different than the manager would have done it. As long as it is only a different means to the same end, the manager needs to be prepared to step back to avoid damaging morale with a micromanaging approach when it comes to tasks versus goals. It also helps to remember that this is a highly valuable skill- and confidence-building process for the team. With each successful project, the quality of the product and team process will grow. The manager is freed to take on other work.

Instead of making all decisions and controlling the work flow, the manager is carefully observing and coaching as needed. Prior to giving up control, managers have, however, guided the creation of shared vision, trust, and excellent communication. Staff are able to talk freely about their progress, ask for guidance or support as needed, and learn continuously as they take on each new responsibility.

COORDINATE INDIVIDUAL WORK PLANS WITH ORGANIZATIONAL GOALS

Employee productivity and empowerment are optimal when individuals perceive their personal and professional goals as compatible with the objectives of the organization. Staff are motivated by their sense of self-worth and contribution. This is also a compelling argument for the manager's role in maintaining clear boundaries in part through a continuous cycle of performance planning, evaluation, and feedback.

Think carefully about how to help staff understand roles and boundaries especially if your organization is migrating away from an autocratic or hierarchical management approach. Although it is exciting to anticipate working in teams with individuals having greater latitude, there is risk of misunderstanding and bad feelings if managers and supervisors are unclear about the scope of employees' work. Thus clear job descriptions, policies, procedures, and guidelines are important (*see* figure 6-1).

Libraries help staff understand roles and responsibilities many different ways:

New employee orientation

Posting core competencies for various job classifications

Making organization charts available for staff

Formal or informal communication guidelines

Illustrating how each individual's work flow affects other employees and the library as a whole

Policy and procedure manuals

Performance planning and review process

Patron feedback system available for all to see

Library mission, goals, objectives, and progress reports available to all

Mentoring and coaching

INFORMATION CONDUIT

Sharing information is a critical role of the manager in the empowered organization. It has been said that there is no such thing as too much information. People can choose whether to take advantage of it, but the availability sends a powerful message.

FIGURE 6-1   Benefits of Role Clarity

Role clarity helps all library employees understand how

> their roles are defined by the library,
>
> that role is translated into a job classification,
>
> the role and classification relate to the goals of the library,
>
> individuals are recruited and hired, and
>
> individual and group performance are evaluated.

The library and individuals benefit from role clarity as employees

> gain an understanding of personal contribution to organizational goals;
>
> minimize stress by understanding expectations;
>
> maximize performance through feedback and evaluation;
>
> see opportunities for job enrichment;
>
> increase job satisfaction, decrease anxiety, and improve self-esteem; and
>
> avoid confusion created by the empowerment process.

Information is the key to responsibility and trust in an empowered library. Library employees with information are compelled to act responsibly.

The tremendous growth in the amount of information available to all is bringing down walls all over the world. Those of us in the information business know better than many that information cannot be controlled. Withholding information carries many messages, including those of lack of trust and respect.

Also important, the availability of information helps reduce hierarchical thinking. Library managers share information with staff in a wide variety of ways including but not limited to the following:

Library intranet

All-agency memos and other print materials

E-mail and telephone

Formal and informal meetings and presentations

Small group discussions, formal and informal

Training and learning opportunities

Social and community events

In the area of information sharing, one of the most important things a manager can do is to create and support a learning environment. This includes honesty and trust so that staff feel comfortable asking questions, taking responsibility for mistakes, and being open to continuous learning and professional growth.

COACHING

What is coaching? In *Coaching in the Library,* Ruth Metz defines coaching as "the skillful and purposeful effort by one individual to help another achieve specific performance goals. The coach facilitates the player's attainment of the player's goals."[2] The coach can help you focus, clarify goals, identify and resolve challenges, and be your best at all times. The coach is by your side as you work toward your objectives. Over time, a coach comes to understand how you think, how you work best, and what your key strengths are.

The organization chart need not dictate coaching relationships. That is, coaching relationships can be boss to subordinate but also peer to peer, subordinate to boss, between people in different work groups, and also between people in different organizations. The most important element of coaching involves defining and meeting the needs of the coachee. Organizations increasingly hire professional coaches to supplement internal organizational effectiveness efforts.

When is coaching needed? Situations that cause people to seek out a coach include times when the individual

feels indecisive or stuck;

has a desire to improve;

is taking on a new task or responsibility;

feels frustrated or confused;

wants advice, assistance, feedback, or support; or

is unclear about his or her career path.

Can coaches seek out individuals rather than vice versa? Yes, but certain conditions need to exist before a coaching relationship can be established. Those conditions include building rapport and a trusting, nonjudging relationship. It is unlikely the player or coachee will be willing to enter into a coaching relationship unless that context exists.

Given that environment, the reluctant coachee might be gently coaxed into trying a coaching relationship through skillful open-ended questioning. Effective questioning demonstrates the coach is interested, has respect for the individual, and is willing to listen. Questions also solicit information, ideas, input, and recommendations. They can help the coachee gain confidence in his or her own thinking process. Skillful questions help focus on solutions and the future rather than the past. Asking questions often helps the other person think through issues and possible solutions. Sample questions follow:

What do you think about it?

What other things should be considered?

How would you resolve this?

What are the most important criteria?

What are the biggest challenges?

Once rapport and trust have been established, the use of effective questioning, versus instructing or telling, helps people open up. It facilitates learning, creativity, and understanding. It enables people to own their own ideas and often come up with their own conclusions rather than trying to implement a solution that is not well suited to their particular style.

PROVIDING PERFORMANCE FEEDBACK

Chapter 2 discussed the value of ongoing feedback as a key component of personal mastery and continuous learning. The manager plays an essential role in setting the stage for feedback in the work environment. Managers model receiving and giving regular trustworthy feedback in a psychologically safe, trusting environment they have helped create and nurture. The manager can also demonstrate the value of seeking out feedback for continuous learning (*see* figure 6-2).

If giving and receiving feedback is new for the work group or the organization, preparation through training and practice could make the transition to a feedback-rich environment a less-stressful experience.

STRATEGIC PLANNING

Although it is important that all staff in the library play a role in formulating the strategic plan or shared vision, it is likely that library managers initiate and lead the effort. Library leaders need to be present to talk with and mentor employees throughout the process as well as to facilitate the work flow. Involving staff and gaining group commitment is also the work of library managers. For specifics on developing the shared vision, refer to chapter 5.

FIGURE 6-2　Guidelines for Giving Feedback

Guideline	For example, say ...	Rather than ...
Be clear and specific and avoid generalizations.	When you talked about the collection policy in the meeting, I didn't understand your point about how it impacts the work flow.	We've got to talk about your presentation style, soon.
Emphasize the positive—the receiver will find it easier to hear feedback if he or she knows the giver also notices strengths.	I liked the way you built a case for emphasizing materials selection. When you shifted to work flow, I got a little lost.	Your bit about work flow was impossible to understand.
Concentrate on behavior rather than the person.	I think it would have been easier to control the group if you'd held the questions until the end.	Sometimes I worry about your judgment.
Focus on behavior that can be changed.	Additional preparation would have been helpful.	You come across as being unsure of yourself.
Describe; don't evaluate.	The font size made it difficult to read.	The third slide was worthless.
Use "I" statements. This is often called owning the message.	When you explained number 2, I didn't understand.	People say they have trouble understanding you.
Avoid giving advice. Help the person better understand the issue and actions that will address it.	Could slides be simplified? I struggled to follow some parts of the presentation.	If I were you, I'd sign up for the PowerPoint class, soon.

PRODUCT DEVELOPMENT AND OUTREACH

Library leaders are often in a unique position to learn about potentially significant innovation at other libraries or other organizations that could have a positive impact on their institutions. In the empowered library, leaders are not so overwhelmed with the day-to-day operating decisions that they cannot take the time to investigate new developments with the thought of bringing best practices back to their institutions. Examples of areas where innovation may be helpful include information technology, customer service, materials processing, and adult programming.

Library managers can take on leadership roles in state, regional, or national library associations or in local civic organizations. They can serve as information literacy outreach ambassadors in the community. Another role is educating funding sources about the library's services and programs. All of these activities ultimately benefit the library, as they are part of the learning and leadership development processes.

In some instances, library leaders are in a unique position to gather information related to how well the library is meeting the needs of their customers. This can take place through community involvement, participation in library outreach events, surveys, focus groups, and other feedback mechanisms. New, unmet customer needs are discovered this way.

EMPLOYEE TRAINING AND DEVELOPMENT

Library managers and supervisors can also take the lead in helping establish priorities for the organization's employee training and development effort. This does not necessarily mean managers deliver training, though they are powerful role models and well suited to that role. Managers are in a unique position to understand the developmental needs of individuals and teams in their work group by way of observation and conversation with staff.

In thinking about staff learning it helps to remember that adults bring personal experience to any learning activity. Life experience is the core of an adult's sense of self. New learning and understanding come as personal discovery in the context of one's life experience. Adult learners need to be free to compare and explore new ideas based on their personal life perspective. Often, the incentive to learn something new comes from the need to be more effective in some aspect of life. Thus adult learning tends to be just-in-time learning. That is, they are ready to learn when they need to know something.

Effective adult learning provides opportunities for discussion and practice. Adult learners may experience internal or external resistance to change. If issues are presented as universal truths, the adult may spend an excessive amount of time searching his or her experience for events that prove otherwise.[3]

Leaving ultimate responsibility for determining direction for training and development effort to the human resource department or to trainers is potentially problematic primarily because it can be interpreted by staff to mean employee development is not supported or taken seriously by senior leaders. It can be viewed as a nonessential activity.

Library managers can ensure that appropriate outcomes, performance expectations, and measurement processes are built in to the library's training and development efforts. The continuous professional growth of all library staff is essential not only for an empowered library but also for the long-term survival of the library.

Leadership development is an important part of the manager's role and includes succession planning, mentoring, and special development assignments for staff. It may be helpful to remember that employees need not attend classroom-type training or conferences to learn. This can be accomplished through online tutorials, videotapes or audiotapes, informal coaching, online discussion groups, weblogs, one-on-one support, and other communities-of-practice types of learning. These deployment methods are especially well suited to the needs of adult learners.

Including learners in training and development planning increases ownership. Also, learners are well suited to realizing and understanding their own personal development needs. Managers should consider visiting the learner on a regular basis to provide affirmation and support as well as give feedback. They can also lend budget support and oversight for the organization's learning needs.

ACQUIRING RESOURCES

Managers play a major role in acquiring resources for the organization. This includes all aspects of funding and budgeting. Resources may also be information, expertise, or skills needed to accomplish some aspect of the library's mission. Figure 6-3 offers ideas on where to find external expertise.

In specific situations, a manager may seek out an external consultant as an organizational resource. Examples include executive coach, grant writer, strategic planner, and technology expert. Some situations where consultants may be needed follow:

A lack of expertise exists in the area of need.

The need is short term.

Previous attempts to meet this need were unsuccessful.

Library managers disagree about how to meet a specific need. The consultant provides expertise or facilitation skills to get consensus.

Leaders want an objective perspective.

Employees are not willing or able to do the work.

An external entity (such as a funder or board) has made the request.[4]

Ideally, managers help empower and coach staff in acquiring resources through mentoring in problem solving and consensus building. The manager may also need to help pave the way or remove barriers by working with other senior leaders to support individuals and teams who are working to accomplish resource acquisition goals. Figure 6-4 offers tips on best practices in using external expertise.

SUCCESS CELEBRATIONS

One of the most enjoyable roles of the manager in the empowered library is providing recognition and reward for work well done. The definition of what specific individuals or work groups appreciate most varies. The wise manager knows the people and work group well enough to determine what is most suitable. Examples include new professional opportunities, flowers or produce from the garden, public celebrations or recognition, food items, poetry, special songs, and cards. One library manager occa-

---

FIGURE 6-3   Where to Find External Expertise

Professional associations offer expertise. Examples include networks of organization design (OD) practitioners, facilitators, trainers, fund-raisers, accountants, lawyers, computer users, and other libraries.

Local corporations with community-service programs may be willing to provide management and technical expertise.

Search the yellow pages of the telephone company or on the Internet under *consultant, volunteer,* or *social service.*

Consider local college- or university-sponsored professors or student projects.

Library consultants and writers often do freelance work.

Other community nonprofit organizations may share expertise, contacts, and references.

Adapted from *All about Using Consultants* by Carter McNamara, available at www.managementhelp.org.

Determine what you want first.

Get internal consensus on what needs to be done.

If possible, arrange in advance for knowledge or skills transfer as a part of the work agreement so you will not become dependent on external vendors.

Plan to get the contractor involved in implementing as well as making recommendations. This will help him or her to maintain a practical approach.

Focus on causes, not symptoms.

Help the consultant understand your library's culture and objectives.

Provide frequent feedback, evaluations, and follow-up.

Adapted from *Making Consultancy as Productive as Possible* by Barbara Davis, available at www.managementhelp.org.

sionally dresses in situation-appropriate costumes and walks through work areas to greet and congratulate staff.

SUMMARY

The roles of the manager in a traditional hierarchical organization and the empowered library are quite different. Before embarking on a new role, it is important for all employees not only to understand the rationale for empowerment but also to have an opportunity to develop a personal vision of their new roles. This minimizes resistance and facilitates buy-in.

As the work previously done by managers is gradually turned over to self-directed teams, the manager must shift focus from command and control to that of coach, facilitator, and troubleshooter. Managers also play a critical role in helping align work plans with organizational goals, serving as an information conduit, and facilitating planning, product development, acquiring resources, community outreach, training, and employee development.

The manager or supervisor also makes certain that employees are appropriately encouraged, recognized, and rewarded for their efforts. Rewards need not be monetary. They should, however, be sincere and appropriate to the individual or group being recognized.

Notes

1. Sandra Nelson, *The New Planning for Results: A Streamlined Approach* (Chicago: ALA, 2001), 38.

2. Ruth Metz, *Coaching in the Library: A Management Strategy for Achieving Excellence* (Chicago: ALA, 2002), 7.

3. Susan Jurow, "How People Learn: Applying Adult Learning Theory and Learning Styles Models to Training Sessions," in *Staff Development: A Practical Guide,* 3d ed. (Chicago: ALA, 2001), 8.

4. Carter McNamara, *All about Using Consultants,* Free Management Library, available at www.managementhelp.org.

Interpersonal and Team Skills

Organizational learning in basic interpersonal and team skills accelerates the empowerment process. We discussed excellent communication and the mechanics of developing shared vision and trust in chapters 4 and 5. The list of essential team interpersonal skills also includes the ability to value and work with individual differences.

Staff come to the library with widely varied interpersonal and group experience. Sources of previous learning in interpersonal relations includes but is not limited to the family of origin, previous employers, religious organizations, social groups, and school experiences. It is interesting to consider that, compared to the workplace of just twenty years ago, today's employees generally represent more varied ethnic cultures.

VALUING INDIVIDUAL DIFFERENCES

Diversity and individual differences are an asset. They introduce fresh perspectives and new ways of doing things. We don't have to look far, though, to see examples of workplace challenges created by individual differences. To name just a few examples, those differences range from learning style, problem-solving approach, or preferred form of communication to ethnic origin and sexual preference. Libraries benefit from employees who possess skills needed for valuing and working effectively with people different from themselves.

Why do individual differences contribute to workplace interpersonal challenges? Intellectually most of us place high value on diversity and individual differences. Challenges often arise from fear of what we do not know or understand. Limited skills and experience working with those who are unlike us may also be a contributing factor. People find comfort and trust in likeness. We may unconsciously seek the company of those most like ourselves. Human beings resist change and continually seek homeostasis. This makes the constant adaptation required for managing individual differences and diversity difficult for people already overwhelmed by substantial changes in the library workplace.

Greater flexibility and workplace adaptation skills can be learned. People we trust give us a safe place to experiment, try new ways of doing things, and ask questions when we don't understand. If the environment lacks critical, blaming behavior, fear is diminished. Thus we can experiment with new behaviors—some of which will result in more effective working relationships with those who do not share our views, style, or background.

An additional consideration in reducing strife created by individual differences highlights the importance of well-designed processes. That is, how often is a poorly constructed or understood process the cause of blaming or interpersonal conflict in the work group? Individual differences can easily exacerbate a faulty or outdated procedure when in actuality the process needs to be analyzed to ensure optimal work flow and minimize conflict.

Individual managers create a trusting environment through establishing general openness and reducing the sense of competition between staff members. Leaders support collaboration and teamwork. All employees, not just managers, in this environment are free to question processes and mental models as well as to suggest that they be reviewed and revised as needed. Individuals, groups, and supervisors who reward supportive, collaborative behavior and team learning fortify the trusting, empowered library culture where everyone is valued.

TEAMS AND TEAMWORK

Teams are one of the most widely used and respected workplace innovations of the last few decades. Do work teams outperform individuals? Teams markedly outperform individuals, and self-managing teams do best of all, according to J. Richard Hackman in *Leading Teams.*[1]

Libraries have historically been hierarchical in organizational structure. Given recent work in improving processes and adopting more businesslike practices, library leaders have begun to emphasize teams as a way to improve the quality of the work life and be more nimble in adapting to ever-changing customer and environmental needs.

WHAT IS A TEAM?

Libraries will not experience the benefits of teamwork, however, if managers directly manage the individual member's work in the team. Team results are achieved when teams do the work. Work needs to be designed either for a team or for individuals. Sending mixed signals about what is and is not a team creates confusion and dilutes the effectiveness of individuals and overall work quality. Results are not optimal when a group is called a team but individuals do the work or when individual team members are managed individually when the work is a team's responsibility.

Work groups who are not teams are "co-acting groups."[2] In a co-acting group, members often sit in close workplace proximity. However, although jobs might be interrelated, the completion of each person's job does not depend on the other people in the group. Group members may perform a process function, such as an aspect of materials handling or accounts payable. In a co-acting group, the manager or supervisor directly manages each individual and his or her work.

In addition to having work appropriate for a team rather than an individual, team membership constancy is also critical. Stable team membership allows the group to

gain experience working together;

develop a shared vision of performance expectations;

learn the ideal division of labor among individuals;

acquire a commitment to the team, each individual, and the product; and

learn together, which may also enhance team effectiveness.

Although many factors influence the size of the team or group, it is important to think carefully about team structure. From an effectiveness or productivity perspective, more is not better, as seen in figure 7-1.

FIGURE 7-1   The Relationship between Group Size and Productivity

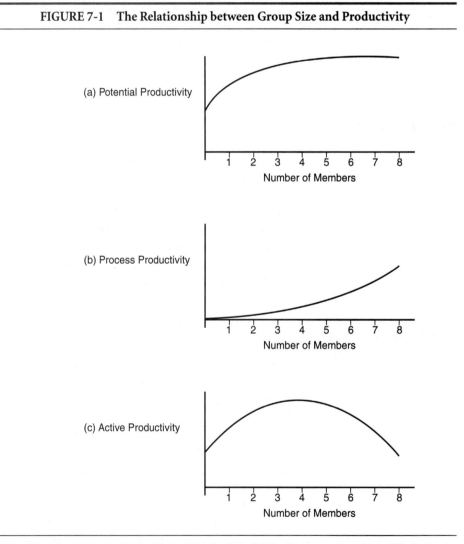

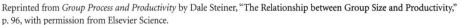

Reprinted from *Group Process and Productivity* by Dale Steiner, "The Relationship between Group Size and Productivity," p. 96, with permission from Elsevier Science.

Regardless of the fact that a well-functioning team should continue to improve indefinitely, a modest turnover of membership over time is recommended as it does keep the team closely aligned with the external environment. Some rotation in membership also benefits the overall organization in that different employees are exposed to the work of this team.

Another essential consideration in structuring teams involves defining what is the team's authority and what is management's authority. Hackman's Authority Matrix (*see* figure 7-2) illustrates the various forms of teams or performing units relative to four essential functions that must be carried out to accomplish the team's work:

1. Setting overall direction
2. Designing the performing unit and its context
3. Monitoring and managing work processes
4. Executing the task

Figure 7-3 amplifies the authority and responsibility of the four types of teams.

FIGURE 7-2   Hackman's Authority Matrix

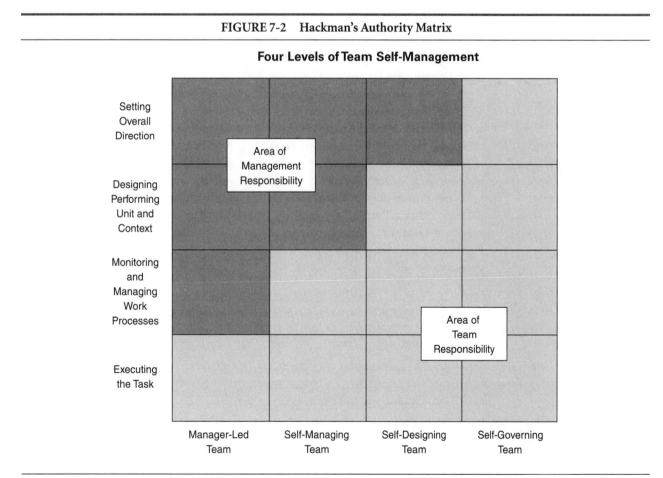

Four Levels of Team Self-Management

Adapted from J. Richard Hackman, "The Psychology of Self-Management in Organizations," in M. S. Pallak and R. Perloff, eds., *Psychology and Work: Productivity, Change, and Employment* (Washington, D.C.: American Psychological Assn., 1986), 85–136.

FIGURE 7-3   Authority Alignment in Teams

Team Type	Authority and Responsibility of Manager and Team
Manager-Led	Manager sets direction, designs team, and monitors work Team executes task
Self-Managed	Manager sets direction and designs team Team monitors/manages work and executes task
Self-Designed	Manager sets overall direction Team is self-designed. Members monitor and manage work in addition to executing task
Self-Governed	Team has full responsibility for all functions

Adapted from *Leading Teams: Setting the Stage for Great Performances* by J. Richard Hackman (Boston: Harvard University Pr., 2002), 51–54.

A good sense of direction not only gives the team purpose and meaning but it also motivates, inspires, and focuses individuals. Each person's distinct capabilities are utilized. Even with strong direction there will always be some uncertainty about how the work is best done. Given shared vision and good team skills, however, members will be able to choose the best alternative for accomplishing their task. Also important, group members will teach and assist those who are still learning a specific aspect of the work.

Hackman characterizes the attributes of good direction as a key to team effectiveness. This direction is challenging, clear, and consequential. Challenging direction energizes individuals and results in a strong collective motivation to perform successfully. Clear direction focuses members on the purpose while aligning the strategy with it. Direction that is consequential employs talents of members and reinforces use of all members' knowledge and skill (*see* figure 7-4).[3]

Given the importance of good direction, should the originator of the team also provide specific direction on the means the team needs to use to achieve the ultimate purpose? Hackman says, "To foster self-managing, goal-directed work, those who create teams should be insistent and unapologetic about exercising their authority to specify end states but equally insistent about not specifying the details of the means by which the team is to pursue those ends." He clearly states that specifying means risks performance problems and underutilization of the team's resources (*see* figure 7-5).[4]

FIGURE 7-4   The Functions and Benefits of Good Direction

Attributes of Good Direction	Functions	Benefits
Challenging	Energizes	Enhances motivation
Clear	Orients	Aligns performance strategy with process
Consequential	Engages	Fosters full utilization of knowledge and skill

Reprinted by permission of Harvard Business School Press. From *Leading Teams: Setting the Stage for Great Performances* by J. Richard Hackman. Boston, MA, 2002, p. 72. Copyright © 2002 by the Harvard Business School Publishing Corporation; all rights reserved.

FIGURE 7-5   Setting Direction about Means versus Ends

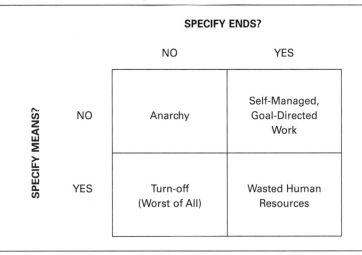

FIGURE 7-5   Setting Direction about Means versus Ends

Thus the primary role of managers is to provide structure, make certain the team is supported by the organization, and offer coaching as needed. As Hackman points out, having "clear purposes with plenty of latitude to decide how to pursue them [is] *the recipe for empowerment.*"[5]

Team and individual learning require ongoing feedback and information about the results of the group's work. When a team receives feedback, members can discuss what was effective as well as what needs improvement. Individual members help other members interpret and understand issues more fully. If the group environment is trusting and supportive, individuals will be better able to examine closely reasons for success and failure.

The manager or coach helps create an environment of psychological safety so team members see every experience as an opportunity for team learning and continuous improvement. Think for a minute about the effectiveness of groups who seek continuous feedback for ongoing self-correction versus those for whom managing small amounts of feedback requires a tremendous amount of energy and time.

In addition to supporting the team's ability to work effectively with feedback, the manager also has a significant impact on task structure. Well-designed tasks attract people and enhance existing internal work motivation. For example, projects designed to directly relate to specific interests of members have a greater likelihood of tapping into members' internal motivation. Consider a group of library employees who need to learn project management skills and are especially interested in serving teens. The manager may be able to facilitate a higher degree of team engagement by structuring a task related to serving teens that also requires learning new project management skills.

The manager also seeks methods of helping members link team behavior to team outcomes. Praise and recognition are consequences of excellent team performance. Rewards need not involve spending money. Although each individual is motivated by different rewards, in general most people appreciate sincere expressions of gratitude and public or private recognition.

The manager also provides process coaching to build teamwork and effective use of team resources. Often, a manager's well-timed, thought-provoking question directed to a team can result in members fine-tuning their work process. Managers provide guidance but not indefinitely. They cannot make the team great, but they can encourage the team to foster self-management ability and increase the chances of members taking advantage of favorable conditions.

TEAM SKILL TRAINING

A great deal of print and other material is available for learning new skills that support the work of teams. A few of those skills follow:

Problem identification process

Brainstorming

Problem solving, including identifying subgoals and understanding the relationship among the parts of the issue

Practice in seeing issues from a fresh perspective

Researching information and data

Critical path analysis, decision trees, and forced field analysis

Statistical analysis

Project management

Forced field analysis

SWOT analysis—analyzing strengths, weaknesses, opportunities, and threats

The manager may want to consider finding a trained facilitator or consultant to work with the team to build team and problem-solving skills. In "Implementing Team Management in the Modern Library," Katherine W. Hawkins talks about *the new organization paradigm* and its components:

All members are responsible for effective team functioning.

Power and decision-making authority are shared by team members; the manager relinquishes control as appropriate.

Focus is balanced on task and social maintenance behaviors.

Task responsibilities are defined in response to changes in task demands.

Creative decision making is encouraged over programmed decision making.

Communication is lateral and vertical.[6]

There are a variety of roles for team leaders (*see* figure 7-6). Transitioning managers and supervisors to a team leader role is a complex process that will be enhanced by both theory and skills training. Issues to consider follow.

It may be perceived as a loss of status.

The new role may be unclear.

Individuals may fear job elimination.

The team leader role may not be modeled by other managers.

Team leader and facilitation skill training may be appropriate.

FIGURE 7-6   Additional Team Leader Roles

Hosting patron, board member, or politician visits

Facilitating networking by introducing team members to external contacts

Buffering team from management pressure

Sponsoring joint vendor-team projects

Gathering or evaluating marketing or external environment trends

Anticipating technology shifts

Building communication linkages

Bringing in customer or stakeholder feedback

Forging alliances in the community

Troubleshooting problems between teams

Bringing in technical training

Brokering team members out to community service

Evaluating services in other libraries

Bringing in community members to discuss services

Skills required to be an effective team leader include the ability to

articulate a vision that creates energy and enthusiasm in others;

manage by principle as well as policy;

facilitate necessary tools, information, and resources;

serve as a barrier buster—opening doors and running interference;

analyze the big picture and translate changes in the external environment to opportunities for the organization;

coach, teach, and help others develop their potential;

maintain appropriate authority balance; and

serve as a role model in "walking the talk."

SUMMARY

Conditions necessary for empowered teams require team leaders to facilitate both individual and team effectiveness. This is done by focusing on employee development and learning. Team leadership is not permissive or passive management. Leaders build organization strength through helping employees solve problems and make decisions for themselves. The role requires constraint, patience, and delegation as well as emotional intelligence and maturity.

Notes

1. J. Richard Hackman, *Leading Teams: Setting the Stage for Great Performances* (Boston: Harvard Business School Pr., 2002), 233.

2. Ibid., 42–43.

3. Ibid., 73.

4. Ibid., 74–75.

5. Ibid., 82.

6. Katherine W. Hawkins, "Implementing Team Management in the Modern Library," *Library Administration and Management* (winter 1990): 23.

Emotional Intelligence

Empowerment and sustained library excellence are achieved through a cycle of continuous innovation and discipline. Employees collectively pursue growth through team learning. The organization as a whole, rather than a few senior managers, feels a shared sense of excitement in exceeding and excelling. Strong interpersonal relations between and within teams are critical to make this a reality (*see* figure 8-1).

The importance of emotions in the workplace is receiving more attention in recent years than it did in the past. As we evolve to a team-based workplace, we need staff commitment and passion. We want full engagement of employees' brains as well as their hearts.

Emotional intelligence in staff keeps the library relevant and vital. It is essential for harmony and maximum workplace productivity. Based primarily on the work of Daniel Goleman, emotional intelligence domains (*see* figure 8-2) are comprised of the following personal and social competencies:

Self-awareness

Self-management

Social awareness

Relationship management[1]

The core of emotional intelligence is awareness of one's emotions. If we are self-aware, we are better able to express feelings appropriately or put them aside if it is necessary in specific situations. Building skills in managing emotions results in the ability not to react to strong impulses generated by emotions such as anger or fear. For example, rather than lash out at a colleague in anger, we are able to momentarily consider what is causing our anger or the possible reason the colleague may have made a comment that generated a strong negative reaction in us. Having done this, we can make a conscious choice about how we respond.

Acting on impulses created by strong emotions often results in behavior that causes us to temporarily derail emotionally. Thus we may mismanage a relationship.

FIGURE 8-1   Quiz: What's Your EQ at Work?

Answering the following twenty-five questions will allow you to rate your social skills and self-awareness.

EQ, the social equivalent of IQ, is complex, in no small part because it depends on some slippery variables—including your innate compatibility, or lack thereof, with the people who happen to be your coworkers. But if you want to get a rough idea of how your EQ stacks up, this quiz will help.

As honestly as you can, estimate how you rate in the eyes of peers, bosses, and subordinates on each of the following traits, on a scale of 1 to 4, with 4 representing strong agreement, and 1, strong disagreement.

___ I usually stay composed, positive, and unflappable even in trying moments.

___ I can think clearly and stay focused on the task at hand under pressure.

___ I am able to admit my own mistakes.

___ I usually or always meet commitments and keep promises.

___ I hold myself accountable for meeting my goals.

___ I'm organized and careful in my work.

___ I regularly seek out fresh ideas from a wide variety of sources.

___ I'm good at generating new ideas.

___ I can smoothly handle multiple demands and changing priorities.

___ I'm results-oriented, with a strong drive to meet my objectives.

___ I like to set challenging goals and take calculated risks to meet them.

___ I'm always trying to learn how to improve my performance, including asking for advice from people younger than I am.

___ I readily make sacrifices to meet an important organizational goal.

___ The organization's mission is something I understand and can identify with.

___ The values of my team—or of our division or department, or the company—influence my decisions and clarify the choices I make.

___ I actively seek out opportunities to further the overall goals of the organization and enlist others to help me.

___ I pursue goals beyond what is required or expected of me in my current job.

___ Obstacles and setbacks may delay me a little, but they can't stop me.

___ Cutting through red tape and bending outdated rules are sometimes necessary.

___ I seek fresh perspectives, even if it means trying something totally new.

___ My impulses or distressing emotions don't often get the best of me at work.

___ I can change tactics quickly when circumstances change.

___ Pursuing new information is my best bet for cutting down on uncertainty and finding ways to do things better.

___ I usually don't attribute setbacks to a personal flaw (mine or someone else's).

___ I operate from an expectation of success rather than a fear of failure.

A score below 70 indicates a problem. If your total is somewhere in the basement, don't despair. EQ is not unimprovable. Emotional intelligence can be learned, and in fact we are building on it, in varying degrees, throughout life. "It's sometimes called maturity," says Daniel Goleman. "EQ is nothing more or less than a collection of tools that we can sharpen to help ensure our own survival."

Mending damaged relationships is important work. It is important to remember, however, that it often consumes large quantities of time and energy that could have otherwise been spent doing other work. If we had the ability to consider the resources required for this repair work prior to an emotional derailment, would it cause us to be more aware of how we manage the emotional aspect of our working relationships?

Personal emotional self-awareness also results in our ability to better understand other's feelings. Understanding and relating to the feelings of another is called *empathy.* Empathy for a colleague creates an emotional connection that allows us to vastly improve the quality of the work we do together. Consider the importance of empathy in teamwork, coalition building, and leadership. It is a compelling argument for developing greater emotional intelligence in the library organization.

FIGURE 8-2   Emotional Intelligence Domains and Associated Competencies

PERSONAL COMPETENCE: These capabilities determine how we manage ourselves.

SELF-AWARENESS

- *Emotional self-awareness:* Reading one's own emotions and recognizing their impact; using "gut sense" to guide decisions
- *Accurate self-assessment:* Knowing one's strengths and limits
- *Self-confidence:* A sound sense of one's self-worth and capabilities

SELF-MANAGEMENT

- *Emotional self-control:* Keeping disruptive emotions and impulses under control
- *Transparency:* Displaying honesty and integrity; trustworthiness
- *Adaptability:* Flexibility in adapting to changing situations or overcoming obstacles
- *Achievement:* The drive to improve performance to meet inner standards of excellence
- *Initiative:* Readiness to act and seize opportunities
- *Optimism:* Seeing the upside in events

SOCIAL COMPETENCE: These competencies determine how we manage relationships.

SOCIAL AWARENESS

- *Empathy:* Sensing others' emotions, understanding their perspective, and taking active interest in their concerns
- *Organizational awareness:* Reading the currents, decision networks, and politics at the organization level
- *Service:* Recognizing and meeting follower, client, and customer needs

RELATIONSHIP MANAGEMENT

- *Inspirational leadership:* Guiding and motivating with a compelling vision
- *Influence:* Wielding a range of tactics for persuasion
- *Developing others:* Bolstering others' abilities through feedback and guidance
- *Change catalyst:* Initiating, managing, and leading in a new direction
- *Conflict management:* Resolving disagreements
- *Building bonds:* Cultivating and maintaining a web of relationships
- *Teamwork and collaboration:* Cooperation and team building

Social and personal competencies also help sustain a healthy, productive life. They give us the ability to move through challenging or difficult situations with relative ease and grace. Self-awareness, optimism, and empathy enhance our sense of joy in our professional and personal lives. Emotional intelligence qualities are vital for strong leadership.

Emotional awkwardness is a professional liability. As an example, consider the individual who is not able to manage workplace relations effectively. Because of frequent emotional missteps and derailments, this person must either entirely avoid working with certain colleagues or spend a great deal of time and energy repairing damage done to relationships caused by out-of-control emotions. This handicap significantly affects the individual's and the organization's productivity.

At some point, even the most otherwise-gifted manager's inability to manage his or her emotions can result in liabilities to both staff recruiting and ongoing work-group interpersonal issues. On a positive note, even though employees come to the workplace with a wide range of emotional intelligence, this competence can be learned. Motivation to learn can often be enhanced simply by helping the individual see how these new skills will benefit his or her professional and personal lives.

Similarly, when library leaders grasp the importance of emotional intelligence to the organization's full productivity, they are more willing to devote time and financial resources toward helping staff gain these competencies. Over time, the new emotional intelligence skills will result in the organization's ability to be more efficient, nimble, and innovative. The guidelines in figure 8-3 can help promote emotional intelligence in the workplace.

FIGURE 8-3   Guidelines for Best Practices

The following guidelines represent the best of the Emotional Intelligence Consortium's current knowledge about how to promote emotional intelligence in the workplace. They apply to any development effort in which social and emotional learning is a goal. This would include most management and executive development efforts as well as training in supervisory skills, diversity, teamwork, leadership, conflict management, stress management, and customer relations.

These guidelines are based on an exhaustive review of the research literature in training and development, counseling and psychotherapy, and behavior change. They are additive and synergistic; to be effective, social and emotional learning experiences need not adhere to all of these guidelines, but the chances for success increase with each one that is followed. The guidelines are divided into four phases that correspond to the four phases of the development process: preparation, training, transfer and maintenance, and evaluation.

Paving the Way

Assess the organization's needs

Determine the competencies that are most critical for effective job performance in a particular type of job. In doing so, use a valid method, such as comparison of the behavioral events interviews of superior performers and average performers. Also, make sure the competencies to be developed are congruent with the organization's culture and overall strategy.

Assess the individual

This assessment should be based on the key competencies needed for a particular job, and the data should come from multiple sources using multiple methods to maximize credibility and validity.

Deliver assessments with care

Give the individual information on his/her strengths and weaknesses. In doing so, try to be accurate and clear. Also,

allow plenty of time for the person to digest and integrate the information. Provide the feedback in a safe and supportive environment in order to minimize resistance and defensiveness. But also avoid making excuses or downplaying the seriousness of deficiencies.

Maximize learner choice

People are more motivated to change when they freely choose to do so. As much as possible, allow people to decide whether or not they will participate in the development process, and have them set the change goals themselves.

Encourage people to participate

People will be more likely to participate in development efforts if they perceive them to be worthwhile and effective. Organizational policies and procedures should encourage people to participate in development activity, and supervisors should provide encouragement and the necessary support. Motivation also will be enhanced if people trust the credibility of those who encourage them to undertake the training.

Link learning goals to personal values

People are most motivated to pursue change that fits with their values and hopes. If a change matters little to people, they won't pursue it. Help people understand whether a given change fits with what matters most to them.

Adjust expectations

Build positive expectations by showing learners that social and emotional competence can be improved and that such improvement will lead to valued outcomes. Also, make sure that the learners have a realistic expectation of what the training process will involve.

Gauge readiness

Assess whether the individual is ready for training. If the person is not ready because of insufficient motivation or other reasons, make readiness the focus of intervention efforts.

(Continued)

FIGURE 8-3   Guidelines for Best Practices *(Continued)*

Doing the Work of Change

Foster a positive relationship between the trainers and learners

Trainers who are warm, genuine, and empathic are best able to engage the learners in the change process. Select trainers who have these qualities, and make sure that they use them when working with the learners.

Make change self-directed

Learning is more effective when people direct their own learning program, tailoring it to their unique needs and circumstances. In addition to allowing people to set their own learning goals, let them continue to be in charge of their learning throughout the program, and tailor the training approach to the individual's learning style.

Set clear goals

People need to be clear about what the competence is, how to acquire it, and how to show it on the job. Spell out the specific behaviors and skills that make up the target competence. Make sure that the goals are clear, specific, and optimally challenging.

Break goals into manageable steps

Change is more likely to occur if the change process is divided into manageable steps. Encourage both trainers and trainees to avoid being overly ambitious.

Provide opportunities to practice

Lasting change requires sustained practice on the job and elsewhere in life. An automatic habit is being unlearned and different responses are replacing it. Use naturally occurring opportunities for practice at work and in life. Encourage the trainees to try the new behaviors repeatedly and consistently over a period of months.

Give performance feedback

Ongoing feedback encourages people and directs change. ^Provide focused and sustained feedback as the learners practice new behaviors. Make sure that supervisors, peers, friends, family members—or some combination of these—give periodic feedback on progress.

Rely on experiential methods

Active, concrete, experiential methods tend to work best for learning social and emotional competencies. Development activities that engage all the senses and that are dramatic and powerful can be especially effective.

Build in support

Change is facilitated through ongoing support of others who are going through similar changes (such as a support group).

Programs should encourage the formation of groups where people give each other support throughout the change effort. Coaches and mentors also can be valuable in helping support the desired change.

Use models

Use live or videotaped models that clearly show how the competency can be used in realistic situations. Encourage learners to study, analyze, and emulate the models.

Enhance insight

Self-awareness is the cornerstone of emotional and social competence. Help learners acquire greater understanding about how their thoughts, feelings, and behavior affect themselves and others.

Prevent relapse

Use relapse prevention, which helps people use lapses and mistakes as lessons to prepare themselves for further efforts.

Encouraging Transfer and Maintenance of Change

Encourage use of skills on the job

Supervisors, peers, and subordinates should reinforce and reward learners for using their new skills on the job. Coaches and mentors also can serve this function. Also, provide prompts and cues, such as through periodic follow-ups. Change also is more likely to endure when high status persons, such as supervisors and upper-level management model it.

Develop an organizational culture that supports learning

Change will be more enduring if the organization's culture and tone support the change and offer a safe atmosphere for experimentation.

Did It Work? Evaluating Change

Evaluate

To see if the development effort has lasting effects, evaluate it. When possible, find unobtrusive measures of the competence or skill as shown on the job, before and after training and also at least two months later. One-year follow-ups also are highly desirable. In addition to charting progress on the acquisition of competencies, also assess the impact on important job-related outcomes, such as performance measures, and indicators of adjustment such as absenteeism, grievances, health status, etc.

These guidelines were developed for the Emotional Intelligence Consortium by Daniel Goleman and Cary Cherniss with the assistance of Kim Cowan, Rob Emmerling, and Mitchel Adler and are available at www.eiconsortium.org.

THE EMOTIONALLY INTELLIGENT LEADERSHIP

Emotional intelligence affects how successfully leaders are able to manage themselves and their relationships. A leader's emotional intelligence also sends a powerful message to the organization related to the qualities valued by the organization. Have you noticed how carefully staff observe and listen to not just the library director but all leaders in the organization? Comments such as "Well, she obviously is having a bad day" to "Did you see the expression on his face when he described how the board voted?" tell us that the way leaders manage their emotions has a significant impact on the organization.

People watch the leader even when he or she is not talking just to gauge his or her reactions. Leaders are an organization's emotional barometers. They have a great deal of influence on employee emotions and overall morale. Staff seek support, a sense of connection to the organization, and even empathy from library leaders.

Many employees also rely on relationships with colleagues for emotional stability. According to Goleman, Boyatzis, and McKee, "resonance" is the leader's ability to drive emotions positively to bring out everyone's best. When staff feel good, they work their best. By contrast, leaders spawn dissonance by undermining the emotional foundation that lets people shine.[2]

A team's performance capacity is comprised of the sum of every member's ability and effort. Thus achievement is significantly affected by group members' emotional intelligence. A positive frame of mind is critical to the work of teams. Laughter, optimism, and smiles are contagious. A good laugh and an upbeat attitude enhance the ability for maximum performance. Goleman, Boyatzis, and McKee go on to say that the more emotionally demanding the work, the more empathetic and supportive the leader needs to be.[3]

In *Moments of Truth*, one of the earliest books on empowering frontline staff, Jan Carlzon, then head of Scandinavian Air System (SAS), talked about the qualities of emotionally intelligent leaders:

> The new leader is a listener, communicator, and educator, an emotionally expressive and inspiring person who can create the right atmosphere rather than make all the decisions himself. These skills were once regarded as feminine, an association that goes back to women's roles in the old agricultural society when they took care of family and social relationships in the village. Their intuition and sensitivity to other peoples' situations are traits that are essential for any manager but cannot, unfortunately, be picked up overnight. . . . I firmly believe that, in the long run, men and women alike will benefit from using *feminine* and *masculine* qualities in good combination.[4]

THE LEADERSHIP REPERTOIRE

Resonance results not just from the leader's ability to be a good role model for emotional intelligence but also from the ability to utilize a range of leadership styles to perform sets of activities that boost organization performance. Those styles are

visionary,

coaching,

affiliative,

democratic,

pacesetting, and

commanding.

Although most individuals have a preferred or dominant style, an effective leader is able to use a variety of these styles depending on the situation (*see* figure 8-4). It is important to note the dissonant styles, pacesetting and commanding, should be used with caution. The ability to use four or more styles is an indication of outstanding leadership.[5]

THE ROLE OF FOLLOWERSHIP

How often have you read about a new management practice or organization-development innovation and at some point the author says "and in order for this to be effective in your organization, it must start at the top"? If you find the new idea personally exciting but doubt the concept would be embraced by your director, how does that statement make you feel?

Ira Chaleff served as executive director of the Congressional Management Foundation and was special assistant for organizational development to more than a dozen U.S. senators and representatives. In his book *The Courageous Follower,* he says, "In order for us to attain the empowerment we crave, we must accept responsibility for both our own

---

FIGURE 8-4   Leadership Styles in a Nutshell

VISIONARY

HOW IT BUILDS RESONANCE:	Moves people toward shared dreams
IMPACT ON CLIMATE:	Most strongly positive
WHEN APPROPRIATE:	When changes require a new vision, or when clear direction is needed

COACHING

HOW IT BUILDS RESONANCE:	Connects what a person wants with the organization's goals
IMPACT ON CLIMATE:	Highly positive
WHEN APPROPRIATE:	To help an employee improve performance by building long-term capabilities

AFFILIATIVE

HOW IT BUILDS RESONANCE:	Creates harmony by connecting people to each other
IMPACT ON CLIMATE:	Positive
WHEN APPROPRIATE:	To heal rifts in a team, motivate during stressful times, or strengthen connections

DEMOCRATIC

HOW IT BUILDS RESONANCE:	Values people's input and gets commitment through participation
IMPACT ON CLIMATE:	Positive
WHEN APPROPRIATE:	To build buy-in or consensus, or to get valuable input from employees

PACESETTING

HOW IT BUILDS RESONANCE:	Meets challenging and exciting goals
IMPACT ON CLIMATE:	Because too frequently poorly executed, often highly negative
WHEN APPROPRIATE:	To get high-quality results from a motivated and competent team

COMMANDING

HOW IT BUILDS RESONANCE:	Soothes fears by giving clear direction in an emergency
IMPACT ON CLIMATE:	Because so often misused, highly negative
WHEN APPROPRIATE:	In a crisis, to kick-start a turnaround, or with problem employees

Reprinted by permission of Harvard Business School Press. From *Primal Leadership: Realizing the Power of Emotional Intelligence* by Daniel Goleman, Richard Boyatzis, and Annie McKee. Boston, MA, 2002, p. 55. Copyright © 2002 by the Harvard Business School Publishing Corporation; all rights reserved.

roles and the roles of our leaders. Only by accepting this dual responsibility do we ultimately accept responsibility for our organizations and the people we serve."[6]

He talks further about the need for people in organizations to move beyond the paternalistic paradigm of the powerful leader and the compliant follower. One doesn't have to look far to observe the seductiveness and the pitfalls inherent in the power of leadership. Chaleff explains that our proximity to leaders along with our personal courage are crucial variables in preventing the abuse of power.

J. Richard Hackman tells us that every individual in the organization must learn how to be simultaneously both a leader and a follower, how to attend to one's teams and one's bosses, and how to resist the temptation either to ignore collective directions or to mindlessly pass them along.[7]

Chaleff's concept of courageous followership closely parallels conditions existing in a learning organization as described in chapter 2. Those include systems thinking, personal mastery, mental models, shared vision, and team learning. He refers to the dynamics of the leader-follower relationship as the five dimensions of courageous followership (*see* figure 8-5).[8]

Followers bring unique perspectives, healthy dissent, and creativity to organizations. If the dominant organizational paradigm says the leader is always right, over time, that leader's openness to variety, innovation, and staff empowerment will decline steadily.[9]

Do you know anyone who leads all of the time? All leaders are also followers some of the time. People spend part of each day leading and another part following. For example, the library director may be in a leadership position and holding the balance of power in dealing with subordinates but will be in a follower position in any interchange with the library board, customers, or voters. Thus that powerful individual

---

FIGURE 8-5   The Five Dimensions of Courageous Followership

1. *The courage to assume responsibility.* Courageous followers derive authority from the shared organizational vision and a team commitment to service. They actively seek opportunities for personal mastery and professional growth to enhance their personal satisfaction and their value to the organization.

2. *The courage to serve.* Courageous followers are committed to the work of serving the organization. They take on additional responsibility as needed and watch for areas where their strengths support those of the leader. Courageous followers support the difficult decisions the leader must make so that the organization can achieve the shared vision of its members.

3. *The courage to challenge.* Courageous followers are willing to take a stand, to risk rejection, to speak up, and to initiate conflict when they feel the actions of the leader are either wrong or inappropriate. They value organizational harmony but not at the expense of integrity or the organization's purpose.

4. *The courage to participate in transformation.* If behaviors of the leader or group jeopardize the shared vision, courageous followers see the need for transformation. They support both the need for change and the complexity of the process. Courageous followers are also willing to explore and go forth with their own need to change along with that of the group or organization.

5. *The courage to leave.* Personal or organizational growth may require the courageous follower to separate from a leader or group. If the leaders are ineffective or their actions are detrimental to the organization's mission and if they are not open to transformation, the need of the courageous follower to separate becomes more powerful. The follower needs to withdraw support or even oppose destructive leaders, despite personal risk.

Adapted from *The Courageous Follower: Standing Up to and for Our Leaders* by Ira Chaleff (San Francisco: Berrett-Koehler, 1995), 6–8.

leads and follows a portion of every day. Strong leaders in a follower role can offer an excellent opportunity for observing followership best practices firsthand.

Employees may be reluctant to move into leadership roles because the higher up in the organization the position is, the more exposed and potentially controversial the individual is. The idiosyncrasies of the leader are visible for all to observe and analyze. Leaders often have to take a stand and at times make unpopular decisions. It is easy to second-guess decisions and to be critical of our leaders. To maintain perspective on the difficulty of being a leader, it may help to remember the adage that asks if you had to make a choice would you want to be liked, respected, or feared? Responsible leadership and followership require courage and for all to exercise emotional intelligence.

Goleman, Boyatzis, and McKee ask, "How does a leader create resonance in an organization that is sustained over time? . . . In any large organization there will naturally be some pockets of dissonance. The overall ratio of resonance to dissonance, we propose, determines that organization's emotional climate and relates directly to how it performs. The key to shifting that ratio in the right direction lies in cultivating a dispersed cadre of leaders who will create emotionally intelligent groups."[10]

SUMMARY

The essence of emotional intelligence is awareness of one's emotions, the ability to manage those emotions, one's social awareness, and the ability to manage relationships with others. Emotional intelligence in the library allows work processes to flow with great efficiency as employees are able to manage their own emotions as well as relationships with others.

Despite having a preferred or dominant leadership style, an effective leader is able to utilize a range of styles based on the work to be done. The authors of *Primal Leadership* suggest those styles include visionary, coaching, affiliative, democratic, pacesetting, and commanding.[11]

All individuals are both leaders and followers a portion of each day. Empowered followers stand up to and for leaders. Both leadership and followership require courage and emotional intelligence.

Notes

1. Daniel Goleman, Richard Boyatzis, and Annie McKee, *Primal Leadership: Realizing the Power of Emotional Intelligence* (Boston: Harvard Business School Pr., 2002), 38.
2. Ibid., 20.
3. Ibid., 12.
4. Jan Carlzon, *Moments of Truth* (Cambridge, Mass.: Ballinger, 1987), 36.
5. Goleman, Boyatzis, and McKee, *Primal Leadership*, 53–88.
6. Ira Chaleff, *The Courageous Follower: Standing Up to and for Our Leaders* (San Francisco: Berrett-Koehler 1995), 3.
7. J. Richard Hackman, *Leading Teams: Setting the Stage for Great Performances* (Boston: Harvard Business School Pr., 2002), 90.
8. Chaleff, *The Courageous Follower,* 6–8.
9. Ibid., 4–5.
10. Goleman, Boyatzis, and McKee, *Primal Leadership*, 225.
11. Ibid., 55.

9

Empowered Library Leadership

The higher up the ladder a leader climbs, the less accurate his or her self-assessment is likely to be. Distorted self-perception is caused by an acute lack of feedback. Those who need feedback most get the least. Subordinates often feel uncomfortable passing along anything other than good news to the leader. The feedback vacuum around the leader is the primary cause of *the CEO disease.*[1]

Emotionally intelligent people understand the value of both positive and negative feedback. If trust and good communication exist as part of the library's culture, it is relatively simple to implement feedback as an employee development tool. The characteristics of the learning organization, especially the focus on the interdependency of people in systems thinking, emphasis on personal mastery, and willingness to question mental models, create a library culture where employees are open to the benefits of ongoing feedback.

Old leaders can learn new tricks. Recognition of one's own strengths and gaps helps set the stage for taking action that will result in leadership style improvements, the antidote of the CEO disease.[2] Acquiring new behaviors and thoughts is complex in that it requires reversing many years of ingrained habit. Clearly, motivation, discipline, and a specific plan are needed. It is also unlikely that an individual would be willing or able to carry out a personal or leadership development plan created by someone else as ownership is an important component of motivation.

According to Daniel Goleman, Richard Boyatzis, and Annie McKee, authors of *Primal Leadership,* "Leadership development is a process, not a program. Strong leadership development processes are focused on emotional and intellectual learning and they build on active, participatory work: action learning and coaching."[3] Thus it is unlikely this sort of learning occurs at a leadership development class or conference although those venues may stimulate thinking and ideas for creating the plan. Effective leadership development comes through self-directed learning in a manner consistent with one's personal learning style. A specific plan, with manageable steps for improvement and a willingness to experiment with new behavior, thoughts, and feelings is needed. To review the self-directed learning process, refer to Richard Boyatzis's model in chapter 2, figure 2-2.

Learning and change of this magnitude requires a combination of information, tools, practice, feedback, and support over time. The use of support groups and executive coaches has become increasingly popular with leaders in both the public and private sectors. This resource allows individuals to create and own their own plans and at the same time adds the ongoing support component that is critical to success.

The authors of *Primal Leadership* suggest:

> The most obvious way to correct distortions in self-perception is to receive corrective feedback from the people around us. The reasons people are silent include fear of the other's wrath, not wanting to bring bad news or the desire to appear a good citizen and team player. Giving candid feedback often makes people uncomfortable. They confuse being nice with providing the other with accurate observations about their behavior or style.[4]

In developing a feedback-rich organization culture, it may be helpful to provide staff with guidelines (*see* chapter 7) for giving feedback and even practice on each other to make the early stages of the learning process smoother.

"If senior leaders are willing to talk openly amongst themselves about what works and what doesn't it helps build resonance in their group." The result, according to Goleman, Boyatzis, and McKee, is threefold:

1. Legitimacy develops around speaking the truth and honestly assessing both the behavioral and emotional aspects of the culture and leadership.

2. The act of engaging the process is the beginning of developing new habits.

3. When seeking comes from the top, others are more willing to take risks.[5]

EMPOWERMENT OBSTACLES

Empowerment as a concept is easy to understand. The potential benefits are compelling. Why then are employees the most underutilized resource in most libraries? Several very human factors make creating an empowered library organization challenging.

One important reason is fear. This anxiety takes many forms and is subtle but powerful in its ability to derail progress. One fear is potential loss of control. Many of us were raised with certain mental models about authority figures. They must appear well educated, wise, able to recall information quickly, and articulate, and they must appear to know all the answers and be skilled at obfuscation when they do not. How will we feel if our manager or supervisor asks a question or admits his or her lack of knowledge about a particular issue? What will happen to our credibility among peers if we do the same? Will our suitability for a managerial role be questioned?

There are other common paradigms related to the role of the manager or supervisor. For example, bosses make the important decisions, closely supervise the work of subordinates to prevent mistakes, and maintain tight control over their work group. In part, this fills the need to appear competent and credible to subordinates, peers, and their own bosses. In an organization evolving to an empowered model, it is natural that managers and supervisors might fear a loss of control of their work group. Team learning requires all members to expose some vulnerability for the organization to grow.

Giving up some control and sharing the recognition for good work with subordinates may raise anxiety over employment security in the supervisor or manager. If I empower staff and give up some of the work I previously performed, will the organization still need me? What if the subordinate is better able to do the work than I am? What if subordinates learn that, like them, I do not have all the answers? Although it is easy to understand this insecurity, it can be minimized if staff are part of the planning process. This allows them to see there is no shortage of work or new challenges for the library. That is, because the external environment continues to generate new expectations, managers who empower subordinates to do portions of the work the manager did in the past will be freed to help manage new challenges (*see* figure 9-1).

Fear may also manifest itself in other ways, such as the feeling that "this is not what I went to school to do." In this instance, it may be helpful for the employees or managers to consider how many people they know who are currently doing the exact same work they were trained to do in school. For those over a certain age, the percentage is likely to be very small. This too makes a compelling case for making certain that all staff understand the entire context of internal and external challenges the library faces and the role they play in meeting those challenges.

Another expression of concern is "this is not in my job description." It may be tempting for the pacesetting manager to feel great frustration hearing this comment. It also reminds us of the importance of maintaining accurate and up-to-date job descriptions. These serve for legal purposes, provide a sense of trust and fairness, and set clear expectations, among other uses.

Often, the act of manager and employee taking time to review and discuss the job description together will help solidify rapport and mutual expectations. It may be helpful for the manager to remember that adults like to have a sense of choices and also control over their lives. There are instances when it is useful to help staff clarify and evaluate their employment options both within the library and externally. If done in a supportive and nonthreatening way, this exercise often results in increased job satisfaction and commitment.

Learning the art of the information interview is one positive way for the staff at all levels in the organization to begin taking initiative in better understanding career options. Not only do people learn more about the library and the external job market but they fine-tune networking skills and most likely get excellent feedback useful for their own career planning during the process.

Whether an organization is nimble enough to survive tomorrow's surprises depends largely on whether the leaders, particularly the top team, have the ability to manage their own emotions in the face of drastic change. Emotionally intelligent leaders know how to manage their disruptive emotions so that they can keep their focus, thinking clearly under pressure.[6]

FIGURE 9-1   Five Ways to Minimize Anxiety Created by Shifting Roles

1. Involve work groups in the planning process.
2. Work with individuals and groups to create a shared vision of the new organization.
3. Skills training, such as interpersonal and project management skills, will increase staff self-confidence and willingness to take on new tasks.
4. Staff will feel safer trying new behaviors if organizational trust is present.
5. A culture of team learning allows employees to discuss what works and what needs improvement.

Responsible dialogue about organizational change should include some acknowledgment and examination of the role of stress. The National Institute for Occupational Safety and Health (NIOSH) works with industry, labor, and universities to better understand workplace stress, the effects of stress on worker safety and health, and ways to reduce stress in the workplace. They conduct research and formulate recommendations for the prevention of work-related illness and injury.

According to NIOSH, stress is often confused with challenge. These concepts are not the same. Challenge energizes us mentally and physically. It motivates us to learn new skills and master our jobs. When a challenge is met, we feel relaxed and satisfied. Thus challenge is an important ingredient for healthy and productive work. The importance of challenge in our work lives is probably what people are referring to when they say, "A little bit of stress is good for you." When challenge turns into job demands that cannot be met, the sense of satisfaction turns to feelings of stress.[7]

Although the importance of individual differences and coping strategies cannot be ignored, scientific evidence suggests that certain working conditions are stressful to most people (*see* figure 9-2).

According to NIOSH, some employers assume stressful working conditions are a necessary evil. Managers feel they must turn up the pressure to get maximum productivity. However, stressful working conditions are actually associated with increased absenteeism, tardiness, illness, and intentions by workers to quit their jobs. All of these have a negative effect on productivity. The following worker-friendly policies can improve results:

Recognition for good work performance

Opportunities for career development

An organizational culture that values the individual worker

Management actions consistent with the organization's values

NIOSH discusses two distinct approaches for dealing with workplace stress. The first is stress-management training and Employee Assistance Programs (EAPs). These result in a rapid reduction of symptoms in a short period of time with minimal expense. Disadvantages include short-lived results and a focus on symptoms rather than causes. Organizational changes, on the other hand, deal directly with the root causes but are more difficult to implement.

FIGURE 9-2   Job Conditions Resulting in Stress

Design of tasks, including hectic and routine tasks that have little inherent meaning, do not utilize workers' skills, and provide little sense of control

Management style characterized by lack of participation of workers in decision making, poor communication in the organization, and lack of family-friendly policies

Interpersonal relationship problems caused by poor social environment or lack of support or help from coworkers and supervisors

Work role conflicts, uncertain job expectations, or too much responsibility

Career concerns, including job insecurity and lack of opportunity for growth, advancement, or promotion; rapid changes for which staff are unprepared

Environmental conditions such as unpleasant or dangerous physical conditions, for example, crowding, noise or air pollution, or ergonomic problems

---

LEADERSHIP AND LEVERAGE

Leverage is the bottom line of Peter M. Senge's view of systems thinking (*see* chapter 2, figure 2-1). It involves seeing where actions and changes in structures can lead to significant, enduring improvements. Often, leverage follows the principle of economy of means: where the best results come not from large-scale efforts but from small, well-focused actions. Our nonsystemic ways of thinking are so damaging specifically because they consistently lead us to focus on low-leverage changes: we focus on symptoms where stress is greatest. We repair or ameliorate the symptoms. But such efforts only make matters better in the short run, at best, and worse in the long run.[8]

Can you think of examples where our daily focus on symptoms of stress at your library keeps us from taking a longer-term, systemic view of the issues and making plans to effectively manage them? As an example, consider two alternative methods of managing strained relations between union and supervisory groups. In an effort to appear responsive, the first management group meets often, discusses issues overheard by various supervisors, and posts bulletins and memos several times a week to make certain that policies and rules as well as supporting rationale are clearly spelled out. The union group, ever wary of the motives of the managers, spends hours scrutinizing the written documents to try to understand "what they are really saying" and communicating informally among themselves. Many hours of valuable work time are spent in this process every week that might otherwise be spent implementing the library's plan. There is no end in sight.

Consider the second approach, where the two sides meet to acknowledge and discuss issues creating friction, then agree to work together on formulating a plan to build trust throughout the organization. Both approaches involve significant amounts of time and hard work on both sides. However, while the first approach focuses on dealing with the symptoms of stress with no end in sight, the second approach confronts root causes and promises a sustained improvement in time and a vastly superior payoff for the time and energy invested.

An important outcome of the study of systems thinking is the emerging ability of an organization's leaders to differentiate between high- and low-leverage changes in complex environments. This means organizing details as well as complexity into underlying issues that create an overall picture of the situation and illuminate not only the root causes of problems but also lasting solutions.

"The increasing complexity of today world leads many managers to assume that they lack information that they need to act effectively," according to Senge. "I would suggest that the fundamental *information problem* faced by managers is not too little but too much information. What we *most* need are ways to know what is important and what is not important. What variables to focus on and which to pay less attention to—and we need ways to do this which can help groups or teams develop shared understanding."[9]

LEVERAGING HUMAN RESOURCES

The archetype of growth and underinvestment is another of Senge's concepts with broad application in libraries relative to managing human resources to remain viable in the information business. *Underinvestment* is defined as the organization building less capacity than is needed to serve rising customer demand. He says, "Disgruntled customers go elsewhere, or if there is no elsewhere, as in the case of eroding standards in an entire industry, customers stop asking for what they can't have." The most important customer performance standards are defined as product quality, delivery service, service reliability, and quality of service personnel.[10]

Senge goes on to say that "if all this happened in a month, the whole organization or industry would be mobilized to prevent it. It is the gradualness of the eroding goals and declining growth that makes the dynamics of this structure so insidious. This is the structure that underlies the 'boiled frog' syndrome. That is, the frog's standards for water temperature gradually erode and its capacity to respond to the threat of boiling atrophies."[11]

Understanding the growth and underinvestment archetype serves as an important guide for the organization or industry needing to create its own future. Libraries are enjoying great popularity but are also engaged in the process of navigating an uncertain future while reinventing themselves at the same time. Consider the potential impact of leveraging human resources. How will the level of employee development investment in our most expensive resource affect our ability to meet customer needs in the years and decades ahead?

Senge suggests that all organizations are plagued with a fundamental problem of seeing the forest as well as the trees but that to keep pace with change, we need to develop the ability to "shift from seeing the world from a linear perspective to seeing and acting systemically."[12]

BEST PRACTICES

Generally speaking, *best practices* are strategies and tactics employed by respected organizations (*see* figure 9-3). As the pace of work life increased in the era of quality and continuous improvement, many organizations realized that to keep up they had to learn from other organizations that did things well. For example, people from the private and public sector went to Memphis in the early days of Federal Express to learn about their revolutionary distribution system. Similarly, organizations looked to Nordstrom for lessons in customer service.

Library veterans learn a great deal from each other at conferences, on exchange visits, and by e-mail. It is lamentable, however, to hear library professionals suggest they have nothing to learn from business or other public agencies because there may

---

FIGURE 9-3   Best Practices of Jack Welch

Jack Welch's commonsense philosophy transformed General Electric into the most admired company in the world and revolutionized the way business is transacted. His six rules are seen by some as the "best of the best" practices in leadership:

1. Face reality as it is, not as it was or as you wish it were.
2. Be candid with everyone.
3. Don't manage, lead.
4. Change before you have to.
5. If you don't have a competitive advantage, don't compete.
6. Control your destiny or someone else will.

Source: Control Your Destiny or Someone Else Will: Lessons in Mastering Change—the Principles Jack Welch Is Using to Revolutionize General Electric by Noel M. Tichy and Stratford Sherman (New York: HarperCollins, 1994), 15.

be one or two attributes they do not admire or respect. Similarly, there are many best practices business and other agencies could learn from libraries. The challenge then is to identify the area of performance requiring improvement and then seek out and study those organizations that have adapted successful solutions. The more broad the environmental scan, the greater likelihood of creativity and innovation in the solution.

In *On Becoming a Leader*, Warren Bennis advocates "ten factors for coping with change, forging a new future and creating learning organizations":

1. Leaders manage the dream.
2. Leaders embrace error.
3. Leaders encourage reflective backtalk.
4. Leaders encourage dissent.
5. Leaders possess the Nobel Factor: optimism, faith and hope.
6. Leaders understand the Pygmalion effect in management.
7. Leaders have what I think of as the Gretzky Factor, a certain "touch."
8. Leaders see the long view.
9. Leaders understand stakeholder symmetry.
10. Leaders create strategic alliances and partnerships.[13]

SUMMARY

Leadership development is a process, not a program. One of the most powerful ways that leaders at all levels in the library learn and improve is through both positive and negative feedback. It is then up to the individual to use this information along with motivation, discipline, and a specific plan for improvement. Coaches, mentors, and support groups enhance the process.

As the library engages in specific steps for implementing empowerment, managers and supervisors should anticipate potential impediments. Fear, stress, and anxiety are best overcome by involving all employees in planning and implementation. Managers and supervisors should be aware of the issues surrounding their own transition from a command-and-control style to that of a facilitator, coach, and team leader. All employees' willingness to devote their patience and support will be enhanced by their awareness of the potential benefits to the library.

Empowerment comes from fully utilizing and leveraging the discretionary effort of the entire workforce. Investing time, energy, and other resources in maximizing your library's human resources is both common sense and essential.

Notes

1. Daniel Goleman, Richard Boyatzis, and Annie McKee, *Primal Leadership: Realizing the Power of Emotional Intelligence* (Boston: Harvard Business School Pr., 2002), 92–96.
2. Ibid., 96.
3. Ibid., 101–7.
4. Ibid., 131.
5. Ibid., 189.
6. Ibid., 247.
7. National Institute for Occupational Safety and Health, *Stress at Work*, DHHS/NIOSH Publication No. 99-101, available at www.cdc.gov/niosh/stresswk.html.

8. Peter M. Senge, *The Fifth Discipline: The Art and Practice of the Learning Organization* (New York: Doubleday, 1991), 114–15.

9. Ibid., 128.

10. Ibid., 134–35.

11. Ibid., 124–25.

12. Ibid., 135.

13. Warren Bennis, *On Becoming a Leader* (New York: Addison-Wesley, 1989), 191–201.

Bibliography

Afifi, Marianne. 2000–01. "Lessons in the Future of Libraries," *Faculty Forum: The Newsletter of the USC Academic Senate, University of Southern California* 2, no. 2 (May): 3–4.

Avery, Elizabeth Fuseler, Terry Dahlin, and Deborah Carver. 2001. *Staff Development: A Practical Guide.* Chicago: American Library Assn.

Bennis, Warren. 1989. *On Becoming a Leader.* New York: Addison-Wesley.

Bennis, Warren, Gretchen M. Spreitzer, and Thomas G. Cummings. 2001. *The Future of Leadership: Today's Top Thinkers Speak to Tomorrow's Leaders.* San Francisco: Jossey-Bass.

Block, Peter. 1991. *The Empowered Manager: Positive Political Skills at Work.* San Francisco: Jossey-Bass.

———. 2001. *Flawless Consulting: Fieldbook and Companion.* San Francisco: Jossey-Bass/Pfeiffer.

Carlzon, Jan. 1987. *Moments of Truth.* Cambridge, Mass.: Ballinger.

Chaleff, Ira. 1995. *The Courageous Follower: Standing Up to and for Our Leaders.* San Francisco: Berrett-Koehler.

Crosby, Olivia. 2000–01. "Librarians: Information Experts in the Information Age." *Occupational Outlook Quarterly* (winter): 3–10.

Dewey, Barbara I., and Sheila D. Creth. 1993. *Team Power: Making Library Meetings Work.* Chicago: American Library Assn.

Drucker, Peter F. 1993. *The Five Most Important Questions You Will Ever Ask about Your Nonprofit Organization: Participant's Workbook.* San Francisco: Jossey-Bass.

Fisher, Kimball. 2000. *Leading Self-Directed Work Teams: A Guide to Developing New Team Leadership Skills.* New York: McGraw-Hill.

Fountain, John W. 2001. "Librarians Adjust Image in an Effort to Fill Jobs." *New York Times,* August 23.

Fox, Sue. 2001. "Shortage of Librarians Stifling Expansion." *Los Angeles Times,* April 30.

Gershon, David, and Gail Straub. 1989. *Empowerment: The Art of Creating Your Life as You Want It.* New York: Dell.

Giesecke, Joan. 2001. *Practical Strategies for Library Managers.* Chicago: American Library Assn.

Goleman, Daniel, Richard Boyatzis, and Annie McKee. 2002. *Primal Leadership: Realizing the Power of Emotional Intelligence.* Boston: Harvard Business School Pr.

Hackman, J. Richard. 2002. *Leading Teams: Setting the Stage for Great Performances.* Boston: Harvard Business School Pr.

Lynch, Mary Jo. 2002. "Reaching 65: Lots of Librarians Will Be There Soon." *American Libraries* (March): 55–56.

Maslow, Abraham H. 1987. *Motivation and Personality.* 3d ed. Boston: Addison-Wesley.

McGregor, Douglas. 1960. *The Human Side of Enterprise.* New York: McGraw-Hill.

Metz, Ruth F. 2002. *Coaching in the Library: A Management Strategy for Achieving Excellence.* Chicago: American Library Assn.

Nelson, Sandra. 2001. *The New Planning for Results: A Streamlined Approach.* Chicago: American Library Assn.

Orenstein, David I. 2002. "Being in the Library Business: An Entrepreneurship Primer for Library Administrators." *Library Administration & Management* (spring): 83–91.

Pallak, Michael S., and Robert Perloff, eds. 1986. *Psychology and Work: Productivity, Change, and Employment.* Washington, D.C.: American Psychological Assn.

Rooks, Dana C. 1988. *Motivating Today's Library Staff: A Management Guide.* Phoenix: Oryx.

Rossum, Constance. 1993. *How to Assess Your Nonprofit Organization with Peter Drucker's Five Most Important Questions: User Guide for Boards, Staff, Volunteers, and Facilitators.* San Francisco: Jossey-Bass.

Senge, Peter M. 1991. *The Fifth Discipline: The Art and Practice of the Learning Organization.* New York: Doubleday.

Senge, Peter M., Art Kleiner, Charlotte Roberts, Richard B. Ross, and Bryan J. Smith. 1994. *The Fifth Discipline Fieldbook: Strategies and Tools for Building a Learning Organization.* New York: Doubleday.

Tichy, Noel M., and Stratford Sherman. 1994. *Control Your Destiny or Someone Else Will: Lessons in Mastering Change—the Principles Jack Welch Is Using to Revolutionize General Electric.* New York: HarperCollins.

WEBSITES

www.cdc.gov
> *Stress at Work.* DHHS/NIOSH (Department of Health and Human Services/ National Institute for Occupational Safety and Health) Publication No. 99-101

www.cultureworx.com
> *Resource Center: Principles—Frederick Herzberg*

www.eiconsortium.org
> *Guidelines for Best Practice on Emotional Intelligence in Organizations*

www.managementhelp.org
> *Getting and Working with Consultants*

Index

Connie Christopher oversees training, volunteer services, and human resources at Multnomah County Library in Portland, Oregon. Christopher's professional career spans more than thirty years. She has been a public school and graduate-level college teacher, corporate manager, and independent contractor. She has conducted presentations for the Public Library Association (PLA), Infopeople, and the Alaska Library Association. The common theme throughout her career is a strong commitment to working with individuals and groups to enhance their professional and personal effectiveness.